TINA;

FINDING MY WAY...

TOMMY BRADBURN

Table of Contents

ISBN: 979-8-9851021-5-4

Published by Tommy Bradburn. Taos, New Mexico

Printed on acid-free paper.

Tommy Bradburn

First Edition

CHAPTER 1

REMINISCING

The sun was bearing down on Denton and temperatures were reaching record highs. At eight a.m. it was already seventy-nine degrees, but later on today, it would reach ninety-eight and for the month of April that's hot! Of course in Texas it's always hot. This early heat wave has been lingering for two days now but the weatherman has promised a cool down, by the weekend, and Tina was glad of that.

At least there's a breeze today, she thought, as she opened her car door and slid inside. When she started her car she glanced at her house with pride. She bought it last year and it's the first house she has ever owned. She must have looked at ten or fifteen other houses before she found this one, but once she spotted it she knew she had to have it. Her new house is not only beautiful, but it's also in her hometown Denton, Texas. On a good day, Denton is only about forty-five minutes from her job, in Dallas, and that's just far enough from the hustle and bustle of the big city.

Having never dealt with real estate agents in the past Tina was afraid that financing may be a problem. She has several married friends who have gone through this process and they encountered many problems, but she had none of those. I suppose it's true what they say, she thought while she fixed her face in the mirror, hard work and good credit can buy a person anything.

As she backed out of her driveway she giggled when she realized that she didn't completely buy into the concept of hard work and good credit can buy *anything*. Tina has worked hard, for ten years, with Burgers Inc., a national fast food chain, which has 2031 restaurants nationwide. She's worked her way from a mere secretary to the marketing director and for a lady of thirty something her salary of $121,000 per year is outstanding.

I also have great credit, she thought, while she sped away from her house on her way to work. She knew that without great credit she would not have been able to buy her $188,000 home or drive this BMW 3251 so what's the problem she asked herself? I have a great job with a great income, a beautiful house and car, I have more friends than anyone could possibly imagine, I've been told that I have a wonderful personality, I'm thoughtful of others, and I'm told daily, how beautiful I am. So why have I never been married?

Before long, Tina reached the on ramp of Interstate 35, for her drive to the office, and her attention was diverted when she noticed the traffic. This was the only drawback to living in Denton and working in Dallas. The traffic! For her that was okay, at least for today, anyway. The slow-moving traffic would give her a chance to think and for the past couple of weeks she's been obsessed with this marriage dilemma.

Finally, the traffic began to move and as she entered Interstate 35 she whisked her long and silky black hair behind her shoulders, out of her face, and once again her mind focused on men and of her being single.

What should I do? She thought, while she glanced through her rear view mirror before changing lanes. I'm going to find the love of my life this year, somehow, and I'm going to get married and I can feel it. A smile crept across her face while she held that thought in her mind and a warm feeling rushed through her body.

Her thoughts were soon brought back to reality when she noticed that her exit was coming up. She turned her right signal on and she began to maneuver through the traffic and as she reached her exit lane she began thinking of her past relationships. Even though she hasn't actually dated much, the past fifteen years, she's had several intimate relationships. Three of them to be exact.

Tina made her exit and she stopped at the traffic light at the bottom of the hill. Let's see, she thought. Bill was my first love. He was a husky well-built man, with a sexy smile, and I was attracted to him immediately. We had a lot in common, at first, but then we drifted apart when he became more wrapped up in himself than in us.

Once the light turned green Tina changed lanes for her left-hand turn and then she drove under the overpass for her last leg to the office. The traffic was still heavy when she glanced at the digital clock, on her dashboard, and she noticed it was only eight-thirty-five. I'm early today, she thought, and she turned her right signal on to turn into the parking garage underneath the office building. As she did, she thought how nice it was to have her very own parking space. She hadn't had to search for a space for several years now and that was a blessing.

When she slid out of her car, and locked it, her thoughts were drawn to Steven her second love. He was a tall medium-build guy with a great personality. He was the funniest man she had ever met, and charm? That man could charm your socks off, she thought. She dated Steven for about fifteen months and she's beaten herself many times for losing him. Her face was long and tears filled her eyes while she stood in that parking garage, with her keys in her hand, as she thought of Steven.

I loved that man dearly, she thought. How could I have let him slip away? We were simply too young and our careers got in the way. We began talking about marriage, and family, and we both wanted two little girls and we even had their names picked out. Steven liked the name Sharon and I was partial to Heather and that was that. The only thing left for us to decide, assuming they were both girls, was whose name would be used first Sharon or Heather. He said, baby-doll, our first born will be named Heather.

I loved him for that and I knew that our lives together would be absolutely perfect. The problem was Steven didn't want me to work. He wanted me to stay home and take care of our children. Stupid me, she thought, my career had been going great, at the time, and I had just been given the position of assistant marketing director. Leaving my career, at that point, seemed very ridiculous she justified. Then, she admitted, I wish I had. But now, he's married and living in New Mexico.

Suddenly, the sound of screeching tires startled Tina and she realized that she had been in another world. She glanced at her watch and it was eight-forty-five and for more than ten minutes she had been lost with her thoughts of Steven. What a sweetheart, she thought, while she headed for the entrance to the building.

Mr. Watkins, the doorman, was there to greet her. Mr. Watkins is a well-groomed, older-man, whose positive attitude toward life has helped everyone working here to start their day on the right foot. He's a man who clearly loves life and he wants to share it with everyone and he does. "Good morning Mr. Watkins," she said, in a very perky sort of way. "It's gonna be a hot one today. I'll bet you're glad that you work in the shade aren't you?"

"Hello Tina, I certainly am and I might say you look lovely today." Mr. Watkins was standing tall when he made that remark and Tina blushed, as she said, "Well thank you. You'll never know how much I needed to hear that." That statement put a bounce in her step and she fixed a gorgeous smile on her face and she confidently walked toward the elevator door. That Mr. Watkins, she thought, he's a dear man.

There were several people waiting for the elevator, none of which seemed eager to begin the day, but Tina spotted an acquaintance of hers and with her, Mr. Watkins smile, still intact she approached him. "Hello Malcomb, how was your party last night?"

Malcomb was taken by surprise when he turned to see Tina standing there. She had a radiant glow about her and she spoke with such a seductive tone that Malcomb was wondering where she had partied himself. He broke out with a smile of pleasure and put his arm around her waist and gave her a little hug as he said. "It could have been a lot more fun with you there baby!" Tina giggled as she said, "Oh Malcomb, your wife would have a fit if she knew you said that to me." He quickly replied, "Now Tina, you know that she has wanted to get rid of me for years and for you I wouldn't mind in the least."

With that, Tina giggled as Malcomb continued, "When are you going to quit this burger job of yours and run away to Hawaii with me?" Tina laughed as she said, "How about giving me until the end of the year. If I'm not married by then I'll look you up." Everyone began to laugh as the elevator doors opened and others began to file into it. Malcomb said in a loud tone, "Okay, everyone heard that, the end of the year. But you won't have to look me up baby because I'll be waiting on your doorstep New Year's Day.

Tina gritted her teeth and shrugged her shoulders and the oddest expression crossed her face as she said, "Okay. Fine. I'll be waiting for you." Then a nice looking lady, one that Tina had not met before, pushed the button to the fourteenth floor and she glanced into Tina eyes and jokingly said, "You'd better be careful he sounds serious to me." Then Malcomb could be heard saying, "Well, while it is a wonderful thought, the truth is, what would you do with an old coot like me anyway?"

As the elevator doors opened to the eight floor the people inside the elevator roared with laughter and three people got off but as the doors closed silence settled on the group. In order to break the silence, Tina asked, "How is your wife Malcomb? The last time I heard she quit her job and she was going to become a housewife." "Yeah", he said, "She's worked long enough and it's time for her to take it easy. Besides, she needed more time to take care of her tiger." "More like a pussy cat," Tina replied with a playful giggle in her voice.

Finally, the elevator reached the fourteenth floor and the doors opened, as to say, Tina, you're home. She stepped into the hallway and with her back turned toward the group inside the elevator; she raised her arm and wiggled her fingers as she said, "Bye-bye Malcomb." Then she faintly heard his voice after the doors closed and the elevator was in motion. "Bye Tina."

When Tina pushed the unimpressive door to Burgers Inc. open, Sally was already busy with her morning duties. Sally is Tina's secretary and she was hired almost two years ago. During Sally's tenure she has done an exceptional job and Tina has often wondered how she would have made it without Sally.

Sally and Tina have become buddies, of sorts. In fact, during the past several months, they have been out on the town on several occasions especially when Tina has been between boyfriends. Sally is a gorgeous divorced lady who is in her early thirties. She has a playful personality and she smiles constantly. She's about five foot five with beautiful long blonde hair, you know, the kind that men love to get their hands into. Sally has the deepest blue eyes and a slender body that she knows how to drape clothing across. Sally is fun to go out with, Tina thought, and since I'm not seeing anyone right now maybe we should spread out wings a bit.

Sally was on the phone when Tina approached her desk and Sally smiled and held her index finger in front of her face, as if to say, one moment please. Tina smiled and had a seat on the edge of Sally's desk while she watched Sally finish her call. Once she finished, Sally smiled and said, "Oh Tina, you look fabulous today, and I love that dress. Is it new? I don't remember seeing it before." Tina smiled from ear to ear as she said, "It certainly is. My mom took me shopping Saturday and she treated me to it. "Wow! I've got to get to know your mother better. I could certainly use a new dress." Tina eyes scanned Sally's body as she smiled and said, "Honey, if I had that body, I'd never complain about anything. In fact, you'd look great in rags." They giggled a bit and then Sally whisked her note pad from the desk and as they walked back to Tina's office she said, "Oh yes, Mr. O'Brian called from Las Cruces, New Mexico. He said everything looked fine to him but he wondered about the point of purchase materials that he asked for?"

While they walked through the doorway to Tina's office, Sally continued. "Ms. Cunningham, from The Valley Forge Meat Co. called and she needs to know how the promotion, with her meat, was coming along. She hasn't heard from you and she was curious. Then Sally said, "Here's her number. She wants you to call her back. And......Your mother, the generous one," they both laughed, and then Sally continued, "Called and she wants you to call her when you get a chance. And that's about it." Tina said, "Okay Sally, I'll take care of it, thanks.

As Sally began to leave the office, Tina called her name and with a curious sort of tone, she asked, "Sally?" and Sally turned to see Tina's face as she responded, "Yes?" Tina asked, "How do you do it?" Sally dawned a puzzled expression on her face as she said, "How do I do what?" Tina's eyes scanned Sally's hot body as she asked, "How do you stay so trim and slim and always look so healthy and incredibly sexy every single day?" A blush ran across Sally's face and she extended her arm and held out her hand as if she was saying stop and she said, "Wait, wait, wait. I love it, but what are you talking about?"

Tina gathered a serious expression as she said, "You know exactly what I'm talking about Sally. Now, let's put the modesty aside. You're knock down gorgeous and I'm jealous!" Taken by Tina sincerity, Sally responded, "I'm sorry, you're serious, aren't you?" "I am," Tina boldly responded, then she continued, "and of all the days for you to come in here looking sexy and perfect why did you pick today?"

Sally smiled and she walked around Tina desk and she held her arms out for a hug and Tina melted into them. "I'm sorry sweetie I didn't realize. Then she gazed into Tina eyes and continued. "You're pretty hot yourself, and you know it, but if you're talking about weight, and Tina nodded yes, then I work out every Tuesday and Thursday nights at Sterling's." Sally lifted Tina chin to stare into her eyes as she said, "Honey, I'd love to take you with me and we can work on it if you like." Tina nodded yes as she said, "Thanks Sally, you're a true friend."

Sally reached for a tissue from Tina's desk as she said, "Now, let's dry those eyes, we've got work to do. They both smiled and Sally made her way to the door once again. Just as she did, Tina called out. "No calls or interruptions for fifteen minutes, Okay?" Sally smiled as she left the office and said, "You got it baby."

Tina immediately fell into her chair, as the door closed, and she put her elbows on the desk and rested her chin on her clasped hands. She took a deep breath and began to gather her thoughts when suddenly thoughts of her third love, Patrick, entered her mind. Why am I doing this to myself, she wondered? Then she tried to push those thoughts from her mind but it was useless and she could not resist. The thoughts of Patrick simply flooded her mind.

Patrick was Tina's latest heartbreak. Parts of that relationship were difficult for her to forget because Patrick was the best lover that she had ever experienced. She remembered him as being kind and gentle and he knew exactly which button to push in order to send her into orbit. Patrick always had the right words for every occasion. She remembered the lovemaking as being incredible and passionate and hot but it took her a year and a half to realize that, that is all there was to Patrick. Just great sex. No more, no less.

She remembered how difficult it was to give that up but she justified that there is much more to life and Patrick had nothing more to offer. Suddenly, Tina caught herself saying out loud, I certainly could use a good dose of Patrick right now. Then she smiled.

I'm tired of this, she thought, and she stood and moved in front of her full length mirror and she gazed at her body as she said, "Oh my God! I've got to do something about this and I've got to do something about it now! I'm fat and I hate it. She grabbed a hand full of flesh from her waist and she stared at it through the mirror as she said, Hey fat. You better enjoy being there, because you won't be for long. I am getting rid of you. Do You Hear Me?

Tina found a new confidence while she stood in front of that mirror and the determination in her eyes almost scared the fat away. When she walked back to her desk she uttered several times, "Goodbye fat. You'd better enjoy it. I'm getting rid of you!"

Once Tina was seated and she began her work for the day a smile returned to her face. She seemed to find happiness in the fact that fat was her only problem in life and if she intended to find the love of her live this year the fat has got to go. Now!

CHAPTER 2

SMELL OF ROSES

Tina was startled by Sally's voice, through the intercom. "Sorry Tina, but Mr. Ballard wants to see you in his office." Mr. Ballard is the president of Burgers Inc., and Tina had several reports to go over with him this morning. As she gathered her things, she replied, "Okay Sally, I'll be right there. Thanks."

While Tina made her way down the corridor, to Mr. Ballard's office, she began to run several points through her mind which she needed to discuss with him. Let's see. Ms. Cunningham, the television station, burger of the month, our meeting in Boston next month with Samuel Morrison, a perspective franchisee. Suddenly, as she turned the corner, and while she was lost in her thoughts, she ran into Bob Evans. Her notepad, pencil, and all of her papers fell to the floor, and Bob grabbed her around the waist to keep her from falling.

Tina let out a squeal, and was startled, and Bob said, "Tina. I'm so sorry. I wasn't paying attention." They both quickly bent over to gather her things and she glanced into his face with a smile of embarrassment as she responded, "That's okay Bob. It was really my fault. I'm late for a meeting with Mr. Ballard and I was lost in my last minute preparation."

Bob owns his own consulting company, which is housed down the hall, and their companies share the copy machines in the building. He has been one of Tina best friends for the past fifteen or so years, in fact, ever since their college days. Bob has been Tina sounding board through all her relationship problems. He's a great listener, advisor, comforter, and he's always there when she needs him. He's the first and only man she's ever known who wasn't after something and Bob seems content with just being friends. Tina had always respected Bob for that.

When they stood she nervously ruffled her papers, as if to straighten them, and Bob moved his hand to her arm and asked, "Are you all right?" he nervously asked, "Yes. Why?" Bob said, "I don't know. You seem a little up tight." Tina took a deep breath as she said, "No, I'm just a little nervous about going to Boston next month. You know how I hate those trips." Bob asked, "Is there anything I can do for you?" Tina said, "You're too kind Bob but just knowing you're my friend is enough."

Bob looked deeply into Tina eyes, and he asked, "All right then, how about lunch, and we can talk about it?" She dawned a sad expression on her face as she said, "No. I'm sorry Bob. I've got to skip lunch today. I've got so much to do. Maybe tomorrow, Okay? Listen. I've got to run. I'm late." And with a snicker in her voice, she said. "It was nice running into you like this. We'll have to do it again real soon." She gave him a seductive little smile and a pat on his cheek and she hurried toward Mr. Ballard's office. While he watched her walk away he shrugged his shoulders and said. "See ya."

When she reached Mr. Ballard's door she stopped for a moment and straightened her jacket, brushed her hair behind her shoulders, took a deep breath, and opened it. Mr. Ballard was buried in paper work as he nervously smoked his Cuban cigar. She loved the smell of it but she had a rough time with the smoke it created. Mr. Ballard didn't look up as she entered; he only motioned for her to come in. Tina went straight toward the huge leather chair, in front of his desk, and seated herself while she waited for him to find a stopping place.

Mr. Ballard dawned a striking resemblance to Henry Kissinger. He's short and a little heavy set but his two distinguishing traits are his black wavy hair and those black plastic-framed glasses.

Tina admired him for all the great things he had done for Burgers Inc. since joining the company eight years ago. For many years he served on the board of directors at State Bank & Trust, and at times, Tina wondered how he made such a smooth transition between the two. He told her, "It's only decision making. It never changes and no matter what you're doing the methods are the same." Tina partially understood. I suppose that's why he knocks down the big bucks around here and I'm stuck with the small potatoes she thought.

Glancing around the room she could see prestige throughout. An intimidating array of awards were sitting on a table against the wall and above that were his degrees from Northwestern, U.S.C., and several computer courses from the University of North Texas, in Denton. There were several plaques of accomplishment, sprinkled on this wall, including his marriage license. He told Tina, in the past, that his marriage to his lovely wife was his most treasured and astounding accomplishment of all and to commemorate that his license was lavishly framed and hanging in the center of the wall with pride.

Of course, no intimidating office would be complete without a portrait of the general, himself, and there it hung just behind his chair. In the painting, Mr. Ballard is sitting behind his desk with his cigar in hand, as a symbol of status, and his expression is stern. It was the expression of a man who was completely in control of his life and everything that surrounded him. He certainly was that, and more, but Tina had the privilege of knowing the other side of this man of steel. He was also kind, thoughtful, and extremely generous. Those were qualities which many people knew nothing about.

Mr. Ballard interrupted her wandering mind as he cleared his throat and said, "Good morning Tina. You look great as always." Tina smiled, and she quickly replied, "Thank you, Mr. Ballard." It was not in Mr. Ballard's nature to beat around the bush and today would be no exception so he got right down to business.

"Tina, I've been going over the advertising budget, for the Southern California area, and frankly it concerns me. I don't feel that we're targeting the right market. Our funds may be better used if we concentrate on the major markets instead of spreading it throughout the valley. What are your thoughts?"

Thank God, she thought. I'm glad I completed my research last night. She took a deep breath and prepared herself.

"Well, Mr. Ballard. I certainly understand your concern and I agree to a certain extent. But the franchisee's in the smaller towns are demanding local coverage. Their responses to me have been that more local coverage and saturation of their particular market area are healthier and more productive for them."

Mr. Ballard, took his cigar from his mouth and he wrinkled his forehead as he said. "Yes Tina, but you and I have a responsibility for the future of the entire company and we can't be concerned with a few individual franchisee's desires. What is best for the future of the company?"

Tina stood and she began to pace and she realized that it would take some convincing to sway Mr. Ballard to her way of thinking.

"Mr. Ballard. I believe that in the long run the budget and proposal, which I have laid out for you, is best for the company. If the local franchisee's are happy with our performance and if they feel that we are concerned for them their production will increase. In turn, sales will increase which will generate more advertising dollars and eventually that will allow us to saturate the entire state just as we did in Florida three years ago."

"You've done your homework haven't you?" Tina smiled and she nodded yes, "I always do."

"Maybe you're right Tina. When does the final decision have to be made?" "The day after tomorrow," she answered. "Okay, Mr. Ballard said, let's sleep on it and we'll make our final decision tomorrow." Mr., Ballard seemed preoccupied with the figures before him and he mumbled. "Yes. You may be right on that one."

They discussed Ms. Cunningham and several other topics before Mr. Ballard dawned a glum expression and he stared into Tina eyes as he said, "By the way, I'm afraid I have bad news concerning our Boston trip next month. I won't be able to attend".

Tina closed her eyes, for a second, as if to say. Damn it! Then he continued, "Mr. Smith, the founder of Burgers Inc., will be in town on that date and he wants to meet with me concerning several matters." Mr. Ballard began tapping his pencil eraser on the desk and then he continued "I'm sorry, but you'll do just fine."

By the tone in his voice it seemed as though he were trying to convince her that she'd be okay and he smiled as he said, "You're not only the best marketing director I've ever met but you're also the best sales person we have. Just turn on the charm and reveal our marketing plan for the area and you'll sign Mr., uh. What's his name?"

"Morrison. Samuel Morrison, Tina said." Mr. Ballard snickered and said, "That's right. You'll sign this Mr. Samuel Morrison in no time."

There was a long pause and silence filled the air and disappointment seemed to fill her heart while she stared at the floor.
"Are you okay with that?" he asked. Tina raised her head with enthusiasm, in order to fool him into thinking everything was okay, and she smiled as she said, "Well of course I'd love to have your help on this matter but I'll be fine as always." Mr. Ballard responded, "That's my girl. I knew I could count on you."

Before long the meeting was adjourned and when Tina left his office she was in her own little world and deep in thought. While her heart wasn't broken because he wouldn't be going on the trip with her, at the very least, he would have been companionship and moral support. Oh well, she thought, it's not the end of the world. I simply hate those long, dull, and boring business trips. Then Tina thought, I wish that the bad news was that he was going instead of me.

Tina dragged herself back to her office with her tail between her legs but soon she began to fantasize of a new lover and as she did she stood tall. She walked proudly, with a seductive little smile on her face, and she began waving to everyone she passed and saying hello to them. Tina suddenly transformed herself into a carefree but sensual lady. This sort of thinking was new to her and she very seldom allowed herself the freedom to fantasize but she loved the way it made her feel and it was exciting and you could see it in her eyes.

Once Tina made it back to her office Sally was waiting for her and Sally was smiling from ear to ear as if she knew something that Tina didn't.

"Okay Sally. What's up?" Sally cupped her hand over her mouth and Tina knew she wanted to play a game. "I'm sorry but I've got a lot of work to do so you can tell me now or it will have to wait until later. Sally showed no signs of saying a word, almost as if she had a secret and she wasn't telling, and she closed her eyes and shook her head no.

Tina shrugged her shoulders as she said, "Weird." Then she went into her office where she immediately spotted them on her desk, the most beautiful yellow roses. She gasped for air, as she said, "Oh-my." And she rushed to her desk to smell each one individually. She looked up and Sally was standing in the doorway. "Who are they from?" Sally shrugged her shoulders, as if to say, I don't know. "Check the card."

Tina read it out loud. "Samuel Morrison, of the Morrison Company. Anxious to meet with you and Mr. Ballard next month." "That's odd," Sally remarked. "Yes it is. I wonder what he's up to." "Oh Tina, you're suspicious of everything. He's probably just anxious to buy a franchise, or, at the very least to see what we've got."

Tina smelled another rose. "I suppose you're right but he certainly made my day whoever he is." Sally smiled. "I can see that. It's written all over your face." Then she bounced out of the office and shut the door.

Tina had a seat at her desk and while she admired her roses she had her first *real* fantasy. She visualized Samuel Morrison, as a man of about six feet tall and dark wavy hair. He's husky looking but by no means fat. He's a very healthy man of forty with the energy of a man half that age. He has the sexiest smile, with deeply embedded dimples, and dark piercing eyes, which held her in a trance. He's not flirty, but seductive. He's a very confident man who knows exactly what he wants. And I'm it she thought.

Like a bolt of lightning it struck her. God, I'm fat! She quickly reached toward the intercom and called Sally with a voice of extreme urgency. "Sally. Come in here please!"

In the bat of an eyelash there stood Sally. "Yes dear are you okay?" Tina smiled and held her hand out facing Sally as she said, "Yes Sally. Do me a favor. Walk to the door and then back again." Sally looked puzzled but didn't say a word and she quickly walked to the door and then back again and Tina said. "No, no. Slowly. Seductively. Sexy." Sally smiled and she began her walk again. This time her feminine charm took over and her body flowed with each step and when she reached the door and turned for the trip back her eyes were fixed on Tina with each step. Once Sally returned to Tina desk she asked, "Okay. What's going on here? Are you sure you're okay?"

"I couldn't be better," Tina boasted. "Let me ask you a question? Can you help my body to look like yours? Sally glanced at the roses and her face broke into a smile. "Awe, now I understand. It's the flowers, isn't it?" and Sally began to roll with laughter and then she said, "Of course I can but you'll have to provide the effort." A determined expression crossed Tina face. "No problem but can we start tonight?" "Tonight will be fine Sally replied, I'll meet you at Sterling's at 7:30." Tina nodded yes and then Sally giggled and she left the office.

Tina smiled inside and out and a chill ran down her spine as she smelled her roses, one at a time, and then she turned her attention toward her work.

The next two hours passed quickly and at 1:00 Sally returned from lunch and stuck her head into Tina office. "Hey. Aren't you going to eat today?" Tina glanced up briefly. "Too busy honey I've got work to do." "Yeah, yeah, yeah, but you have to keep up your strength. Never mind. We'll talk about diet tonight. By the way, your mother called again." Then Sally slipped away.

Oh mom I forgot all about you, Tina thought, and she picked up the phone to dial the number. "Hello mom. I'm sorry. I've been in meetings and had so much catching up to do. Can you forgive me?" Tina giggled. "Mom, I'd love to have dinner with you but it'll have to be early. I have an appointment at 7:30. No mom. Unfortunately, it's not a date but can I bring Bob? Okay great. I'll see you around 5:30. Bye mom I love you. Yes mom, I'll be careful on the highway. Bye now."

"Sally, will you get Bob on the phone for me please? Thanks." Tina had a warm feeling inside as she drew a deep breath before continuing her work. She was so in love with both her parents. They were the happiest couple she knew and every time she talked to or visited them she never left them without feeling great.

Her mother, Joan, is a short and very petite lady and Tina always envied that. Her mother seemed to glow with the joy of life constantly surrounding her. Just being around this career housewife could set your heart free. Tina dad, James, is a sweetheart. He has often said, if he wasn't already married, he'd marry Tina and she took that as the ultimate compliment. This silver haired fox is a dentist. He's rather small but lean and stout. Those two are so much fun to be around. Constantly joking and never worried about life's problems. He says problems are created not inherited. If you have a problem, let's solve it and move on.

As she was returning a file folder the phone rang. It was Bob. "Hello baby. Have you run into any more good-looking women today? Ha, ha. I wouldn't dream of running into anyone but you darling." She laughed out loud as Bob told her he's been thinking about it all afternoon and even planning a strategy on doing it again. "You're crazy. Do you know that? Listen. I'm sorry about lunch today but how about dinner? Yes, tonight silly. At mom and dads. No, I don't know what they're having but we could have each other if that's what you'd like." Tina face turned red and she laughed until it hurt. When she finally caught her breath she said, "Listen silly, it'll have to be early. Okay? I've got an appointment at seven-thirty. Hey, that's exactly what mom asked me. No, it's not a date. I'm going someplace with Sally. I'll tell you about it later, okay? I'll meet you in the parking lot at five o'clock. Don't be late or I'll leave you." With a giggle she said, "I love you too baby. Bye-bye."

The last two hours of the day, were hectic but finally, Tina closed the file folder on the last piece of work for the day. She sat there silently, and sighed, while she gathered herself and her frame of mind. She slowly glanced at her clock. Oh my gosh! It's four-fifty. I'd better move it or I'll be late. She quickly returned the folder; she had been working on, wrote herself a few last minute notes, for tomorrow, and headed for the door.

When she passed Sally, she said, "Bye honey, Bob and I are having dinner with my mom and dad. I'm late but I'll see you at seven-thirty." And she continued to walk. Sally smiled. "Don't eat too much and be careful! I'll see you later."

Tina hurried through the door and the hallway was busy with people crowding into the elevators. Tina was busy smiling, and nodding her head, as she made her way to the elevator doors. Just then, they opened and she squeezed in and sighed with relief thinking how lucky she was to have made it on the first one.

The elevator was a bee hive of conversation as Tina watched the numbers of the floors click off 12, 11, 10, 9, and then it stopped on the eighth floor. As the doors opened, Malcomb, and several other people were waiting to get on but there was no room for another body. "Sorry Malcomb, see you tomorrow." And the doors closed and Malcomb simply smiled and waved.

The elevator continued. 7, 6, 5, and then stopped again, on the fourth floor. A lady, in the very back of the elevator, needed off, and everyone maneuvered to let her through, and then the doors closed again, and the elevator continued. 3, 2, 1 and finally to the parking deck. The crowd slowly made its way off the elevator and they began thinning out as they reached the door to the parking garage.

While they filed through the door she could hear each of them telling Mr. Watkins good night and then him doing the same. When she reached him Tina asked, "Mr. Watkins, has Bob made it down yet?" "No, not yet, he replied." She smiled, and patted his pot belly. "Good. See you tomorrow." Then she made her way to her car and she waited for Bob.

The wait was short and Bob walked up and kissed her cheek with his hand on her waist. "Hello beautiful. I made it as fast as I could." "You did great Bob. I just got here myself. You want to follow me over there?" "Of course, but no speeding, I know how you drive and I don't need a ticket." She giggled. "Okay grandpa I'll take it easy."

She started her car and waited for Bob to get into his and she checked her face in the mirror and thought oh my goodness, face, you need help. Then she backed her car out and headed toward the exit and as soon as she was out of the parking garage she checked her rear view mirror and made sure Bob was close behind. It really didn't matter, she thought, he knows the way. The traffic was hectic, as usual, for this time of the day but before long she made it to the interstate and was finally able to relax.

While she cruised down the highway she began to think of her beautiful yellow roses and of Samuel Morrison. She visualized him standing under an old oak tree with his arms opened wide, for her, and she quickly fell into them. His hug was firm and his lips were warm and soft as they passionately kissed. Suddenly, she realized that in her fantasy she was slim and trim. She was sexy looking and very sensual and her silky dress hugged the curves of her hot body. In reality, she was smiling, and taken away, and she imagined Samuel kissing her neck while his hands rested on her hips.

She heard herself saying. "Oh Samuel." And her thoughts were brought back to the highway. She was surprised to find her hand caressing the front of her blouse and her nipples were hard and her face was hot and beads of perspiration had formed, on her body. She began blushing and her fingers grasped the front of her blouse and she pulled it from her body and she blew cool air down the front of it and said out loud. "What am I doing? What's wrong with me?"

She quickly disregarded those negative thoughts and a timid almost sneaky smile crept across her face. She loved the feeling she had as she tried to fight off those feelings of guilt.

Before she knew it her exit was in front of her and she glanced into her rear view mirror to make sure Bob was still following, and he was, and she turned her signal on and smiled.

Many things filled her mind as she continued her drive toward her mom's house and she realized she was mentally going through many wonderful changes which she didn't understand. At the age of thirty-seven she felt as though she was at her sexual peak but had no man to share it with. Tina felt as though she had no one to help her cultivate those fabulous and exciting feeling and thoughts which she had never allowed herself to experience or to explore. Now, her body and mind were beginning to cry out and were on the verge of sexual explosion.

She tried to cool down cramming her mind with thoughts of her parents as she approached their house. Far too soon for her, she found herself turning into their driveway and putting her car into park and turning the engine off. She quickly glanced at her face in the mirror and said. "Goodness." Then she took a deep breath readying herself for reality and she opened the door.

Bob was standing next to her car as the door swung open. "Are you okay?" He asked. Then with a worried tone in his voice he said, "You were all over the highway." "I know goofy. I was cleaning out my console. I never have time to do that unless I'm driving." With both her hands she grabbed his arm and hugged it close to her body as they walked to the front door and she wondered how she had thought of the console excuse so quickly but she was glad she did.

Joan was waiting at the front door for them and she opened it and they walked in. Tina perked up immediately when she saw her mother's face and she gave her a tight hug. "Hi mom you're looking full of energy today." "Thank you dear. I worked in the back yard this afternoon and you know how I love that."

Joan reached to give Bob a hug. "Hello you hunk," she said. Then with a whiney voice, Tina said, "Mom!" Bob's face lit up, as he hugged Joan, and he patted her on the back with both hands as he said, "Thanks Joan. I've been working on it." As he did he looked at Tina, over her mom's shoulder, and he winked.

Tina stuck her tongue at Bob as she asked, "Mom, where's daddy?" "You know very well where he is." in a joking voice. "He's in the study." Tina began walking away towards the study as she said, "I'm gonna stick my head in and say hello."

It was a modest little house but very comfortable and decorated in a way which only Joan could have. One of the three bedrooms had been converted into a study and the door had been taken down and replaced with French doors. While James was not a carpenter he did the work himself and Tina was proud of the professional job he did.

James was seated at his desk and his back was facing the door as Tina entered. She quietly pushed the doors open and very carefully began tiptoeing towards him trying to sneak up on him but James was far too smart for that. After she took three steps, "I hear a prowler", he said. Tina giggled. "Oh daddy you never let me do that. One of these days pretend you don't hear me. Okay?" She walked up behind him and threw her arms around him and kissed the top of his head.

"I'll work on that. I promise." and he moved his chair from his desk and he stood, to get a real hug. He wrapped his arms around her and kissed her cheek and asked, "How's my Cupcake?" "Terrific daddy, how about you?" "Honey, if I were doing any better. . . Well, you know." Then as he starred into Tina eyes, he said, "Now that you're here I'm perfect."

Just then Bob walked in. "Hey James", he said and he reached his hand out for a handshake. James took Bob's hand with both of his as if he were very glad to see him. "Well hello Bob. Good to see you. Listen I've got a question for you." and they huddled around James' computer and he began asking his question. "Well. I can see you two are busy so I'll go keep Mom Company. Have fun." "I'll see you in a little bit Cupcake." Then Bob turned towards her and said, "Keep the conversation light Tina." She wrinkled her face and giggled as she said, "Okay, if I have to."

When she reached the kitchen her mom was busy cooking and Tina had a seat at the bar to watch her. There was a bowl of carrot sticks in front of Tina and she helped herself as she took a bite of one and with an inquisitive tone, she asked, "Mom?" Joan raised her head as she stirred the green beans and she rested the lid on top of them she answered, "Yes dear." Tina was almost too shy to ask, but finally, the words spilled out. "Do you ever have fantasies?" Joan, dawned a surprised expression, and turned to face Tina. "What?" Tina blushed and she realized this conversation couldn't be stopped now. "I've found myself daydreaming, lately, and I wondered if that's ever happened to you. Or if I'm just weird."

Joan dropped her towel on the cabinet and she walked over to the bar and she took a carrot stick. She leaned against the bar; about two feet from Tina's face and she stared deeply into Tina eyes. "What kind of fantasies?" she asked. Tina was embarrassed and had a meek tone to her quiet voice. "You know, sexual." Joan didn't bat an eyelash and a smile ran across her face and her eyes lit up and she held her head high, with pride, and then she responded. "I have." Almost in a confidential manner she moved closer to Tina and she raised her eye brows as she said, "It's exciting, isn't it?"

Tina's mouth fell open. "Mom, I never. . . ." Joan interrupted. "You never what? Thought that an old lady like me could dream of such things?" Tina smiled. "Yeah." "Don't worry sweetie, I only fantasize about your father," and they both giggled.

"I don't understand what's going on with me. Just today I began these fantasies, and at first, they scared me," Tina said. Then Joan smiled and said, "Don't worry about them dear. Indulge yourself. They're healthy and certainly nothing to worry about." Tina threw her arms around Joan's neck and gave her a peck on the cheek. "Thanks mom. I love you so much." Joan stared into Tina eyes and then she blurted out, "I'm happy for you but you really need to find a husband." Tina rose up and said; "Now mom you know I'm trying."

Joan walked back to the stove, to check on dinner, when suddenly, Tina said, "Oh, by the way Sally and I are going to Sterling's tonight. I'm going to get rid this fat of mine." Joan quickly turned toward Tina and with a serious expression on her face, and said, "Now honey. I don't like to hear you use that tone on yourself. You're a beautiful young lady." Tina responded, "I'm sorry. But I realized this morning that I need to lose some weight if I'm ever going to snag a man in this century." Joan giggled as she asked, "You've had a busy day, haven't you?" Tina nodded yes.

"By the way is my jogging outfit still here? Tina asked." Then Joan said, "Yes dear. It's in your duffle bag in my bedroom. I'll get it for you. You get your daddy and Bob while I set the table." Tina walked to Joan's side and hugged her as she said. "Thanks mom. You're terrific." Then Joan said, "Go on now. Get the men!" Tina began walking away backwards and she pointed to Joan as she said, "I love you." Then she turned around and made her way to the study.

As she walked through the doorway to the study the men were sitting in the two huge leather chairs, laughing, and telling jokes. Probably, dirty jokes, she thought. When they saw her face their expressions were one of. Oh no we've been caught. Then James blurted out, "Cupcake?" and he laughed. "I don't think you should hang around this guy very much." Bob laughed and stood to defend himself as he said, "I've only spent too much time with you apparently."

Tina giggled and said, "Alright you two if you can't get along I'll be forced to separate you." They laughed and she moved to Bob's side and she wrapped her arms around him and interlocked her fingers and she began to pull him. "Come on, you two. It's time for dinner." James jumped up from his seat and wedged himself between them and they walked to the kitchen singing "Home on the Range" as they walked to the beat of the song.

Joan heard the racket and she glanced up to see the sight and then she covered her face, with her hands, and she began shaking her head no. She laughed and stared into their faces as they walked through the den and then she said. "You guys are a mess. An absolute mess." Then suddenly Tina, broke free, for a second, and she took Joan's hand and gave it a tug as she said, "Come on mom, join us." Joan braced herself against the bar. "No thank you I've got work to do." Tina giggled as she pulled. "Oh, come on." and she finally maneuvered her next to the others and the four of them stood in a row, like can-can dancers, and they began singing Home on the Range.

Before long, and almost simultaneously, James and Bob began to kick their legs into the air. Everyone began to laugh uncontrollably and Tina and Bob fell to the floor and they laughed. Everyone laughed and laughed until Tina blurted out "Stop it. I can't take it anymore. Please stop." That made Bob and James laugh even more and Joan helped Tina up and took her to the kitchen. Each of them held their belly, in pain, since they had laughed so hard they had tears in their eyes and Tina wiped hers away as she said. "You guys are goofy. Do you hear me? You're goofy!"

The men began making their way toward the dining room and their laughter faded and Bob asked, "What's wrong Tina, can't you take it?" She took a deep breath and tried to compose herself as she said, "I guess not. I haven't laughed that hard in years." Tina and Joan walked into the dining room together with the last bowl of food and everyone was seated. James was at the head of the table, Joan to his right, and Tina on his left, with Bob at the other end of it facing James. Then James asked, "Bob, will you lead the blessing?" Bob smiled and responded, "I'd love to." and they held hands, and bowed their heads. "Heavenly Father, thank you for the food before us and all that you have blessed us with. I ask Lord that you guide Tina, as she prepares for her trip to Boston, and give her the wisdom and strength she needs to do well. In Jesus name Amen.

Tina glanced at Bob, with appreciative eyes as she said, "Thanks Bob." He nodded, as if to say, anytime and then he blurted out. "Let's eat!"

While the food was being passed around James rested his hand on Tina and he asked, "Bob, How's your love life?" Tina blushed and had a glare in her eyes as she said, "Daddy!" Then James tried to right the ship as he said, "Well. I mean. . . .Are you dating anyone special?" Tina glared at James as she said, "Daddy, will you leave Bob. . . ." and Bob interrupted, and rested his hand on hers and he smiled as he answered James. "No. No one special." Then James smiled and said. "Well, you know. . . .You two seem to get along very well." Tina took her hands back and she pointed her finger at James as she said, "Alright daddy. That's enough. Let's talk about something else!"

Suddenly Joan blurted out. "How about them Cowboys?" Everyone giggled. "Honey?" James responded. "They don't even begin preseason until July." Then Joan replied, "Yeah, but it's never too early to start thinking about them. And besides it was the first thing that came to my mind." Tina giggled as she said, "Good thinking mom. At least it changed the subject."

Tina casually glanced at the clock on the wall and she asked, "Oh my goodness, mom is that clock right?" Then, as she checked her watch Joan answered, "Yes it is dear." Tina quickly stood and said, "I'm sorry everyone but its six forty-five and I've got to go. I'm supposed to meet Sally at seven-thirty and I don't want to be late. Then Joan said, "Dear, She'll wait. Sit down and eat." Then Tina said, "Mom, you know how I am. I don't like being late for anything. I'm sorry but I've got to go."

Joan stood and she began putting a sandwich together for Tina to take with her and she said, "Here dear at least take a sandwich with you. "Tina stood as she said, "Okay mom. I'm sorry. Time just got away from me," and she glared at Bob, in an accusing sort of way and Bob quickly said, "Oh no you don't, I never asked you to dance, that was your idea". James quickly agreed as he said, "That's right". Then Tina shook her finger at each of them as she said, "Sure. Go ahead and defend each other. I don't care. Mom knows who started that, don't you mom?" Joan giggled. "Hey. Leave me out of this. I've got a sandwich to wrap." and she disappeared into the kitchen with Tina sandwich.

The men snickered as Tina walked behind James' chair and she hugged his neck and then she said, "Good night daddy. Thanks for dinner. I love you." James responded, "Good night Cupcake. I love you too." Then Tina walked behind Bob and placed her fingers around his throat, as if she were going to strangle him and she laughed as she said, "And I'll see you tomorrow precious." And she bent down and kissed his cheek. He smiled and said, "Good night baby. See you tomorrow."

The clock was approaching six fifty-five and Tina said, "Sorry guys. I've got to run." and she walked backwards, towards the kitchen, and blew them a kiss. When she turned around Joan was standing at the counter putting Tina wrapped sandwich into a paper sack. Tina grabbed her duffle bag and she took Joan's hand and they quickly walked toward the door and Tina said in a whisper, "I feel much better after talking with you about my fantasies mom. Thanks." Joan looked deeply into her eyes and she smiled, as she said, "I'm excited for you, and remember, indulge!" They giggled, and Joan continued. "Be careful, on that highway tonight. Okay?" Then Tina said, "I will mom. Bye now." "Goodnight dear."

Joan stood at the door while Tina drove away. Her smile, and enthusiastic wave good-bye, told Tina how much her mother loved her. What a great family, she thought, as the house disappeared in the distance. She made her way to the on ramp of the highway and she decided to have her sandwich later. Tina was focused on beginning her exercise program and developing that sleek, sexy body, which she'd always dreamed of. Lost in thoughts of how painful the program may be she was determined to see it through at any cost.

Before long she was pulling into the lighted parking lot of Sterling's and she glanced at her clock to find it was only seven twenty-five. She sighed with relief realizing she was early and she parked and grabbed her bag. While she walked to the front door her mind drifted to thoughts of Bob. Fifteen years ago her and Bob had dated briefly. They took a few classes together at the University of North Texas, but after several dates, they realized that their relationship was better suited for friendship than as lovers. Since that day their friendship had blossomed into something she couldn't describe in words. It's not romantic, she thought, but it's much closer than simple friendship.

Once she walked inside, and then to the counter, she asked if Sally had arrived yet but she hadn't so Tina decided to have a seat, across the way, while she waited for her. Bob is much closer than a brother, she thought, as she sat on the large woolen sofa. I don't know but I do love our relationship and I don't know what I'd ever do without him. A warm smile ran across her face, while she thought, he's my sweetheart. And I never want to change that.

Suddenly, Sally was standing in front of her and she could see that Tina was lost in thought. Sally smiled and she tapped Tina's leg, with her foot, as she said, "Hello. Is anybody there?" Tina looked up and blushed as she replied, "Gosh Sally, you startled me." Sally laughed and said, "Well, I can see that where has your mind been? Judging by the expression on your face you must have been in heaven." They giggled, and Tina stood, and picked up her bag, and took Sally's arm. As she said, "Come on Sally. I've got to lose this fat!"

After the aerobics class Tina was sweating, and out of breath and her and Sally had a seat in the locker room. Sally leaned towards Tina and said, "Don't worry, It'll get easier." Then she smiled as she said, "Now, about your diet and you'll love this. You can eat anything your heart desires but when you do eat teach yourself to eat less." Tina's eyes were trained on Sally, while she spoke, and Tina took it all in and she intended to follow Sally's instructions to the letter.

Sally said, "You see. Your stomach is stretched now because you've trained it to be that way." Then Sally stood, and began to undress for her shower as she continued, "But, as you eat less, your stomach will need less. Does that make any sense?"

Tina shook her head yes as she said, "Believe me, the last thing in the world I'm thinking of right now is food."

And her eyes were glued to Sally's body as Sally pulled her sweatshirt over her head then Sally stared into Tina's eyes as she said, "I know you're not hungry now but when you are, remember to eat less. "Sally pulled her shorts down to her feet and she stepped out of them. Tina's eyes had a field day as she scanned Sally's body as she stood nude. Sally's breasts were firm and her tummy was tight. Her body was absolutely perfect and she looked delicious.

"How long?" Tina asked. Sally dawned a puzzled expression and asked, "How long what?" Tina sheepishly pointed to Sally's beautiful body and asked, "How long before I look like that?" Sally blushed, bent down to kiss Tina's cheek, and she whispered, "Soon dear just keep after it."

Sally asked, "I'm going to take a shower now, are you coming?" Tina said, "No. I'll wait until I get home. But I'll see you in the morning." Sally jokingly said, "Well okay then just be that way." Then Sally walked away and Tina's eyes watched every step she took. Wow, she thought. That woman is something else and that's exactly how I want to look and carry myself. Just as Sally was entering the shower she turned her head towards Tina and she smiled and held her hand above her head and she wiggled her fingers then she disappeared into the steam.

Tina felt good about the workout and as she picked up her things and headed for the car she decided to practice Sally's sexy walk. There she was, in her sweats, carrying her duffle bag, and trying to walk sexy. She was a sight but as she passed the front counter she could have cared less what anyone was thinking.

When Tina finally made it home she made her way to the bedroom where she dropped her bag next to a sitting chair and she went to the bathroom to start her shower. She walked back to the bedroom and stood next to her bed where she began to undress and then she stood naked in front of the mirror.

A sad expression covered her face as she shook her head no and she thought. You've got a long way to go baby before you come close to Sally's gorgeous body. She turned sideways and continued to stare into the mirror and she thought. An awful long way! She began to stare at her face and then into her eyes but the light was dim and she moved toward the bathroom mirror.

You're beautiful, she thought, you really are. She gently reached up to pull her long and silky black hair to the front of her body and it rested just above her breasts. She looked into those beautiful eyes of hers again which were deeply etched into her face. They were outlined by very long and seductive lashes. Her cheekbones stood out from her face on each side of her petite and perfectly shaped nose which gave her a look of confidence. But her luscious thin lips are what she was the proudest of. They looked delicious and inviting as they stretched across her face and her dimples seemed to accentuate them.

Yes, she thought. You're going to be a very beautiful lady. Then she stepped back to view her entire body. As soon as I take care of this fat. She glanced at her clock and it was nine forty-five so she took her shower, put her gown on and she eased into her cozy bed. The day had been long and the workout had been tiring and she quickly drifted off to sleep.

CHAPTER 3

Happy Birthday Papa

The pain was more than Tina could bare when she swung open the doors to Burgers Inc. Last night's aerobics work out had been more than she bargained for. Every muscle in her body ached, muscles she didn't even know she had.

She wasn't able to bend over or pick anything up and simply walking was painful. It was uncomfortable sitting, or lying down, or driving a car, and it even hurt to breath. The pain was so extreme she didn't want to be in public and she certainly had no business going to work but she did.

When she tried to hobble into her office, Sally turned around. "Good morning aerobics queen. I see you have a little pain this morning." "Oh Sally it's awful. I almost didn't make it to the elevator." Sally walked over to her and she wrapped her arm around her and helped her to her office.

Sally eased her into her seat as she said, "Honey, I knew you were over doing it last night." Tina looked up at Sally and replied, "Yeah well, it hurts, but it feels good at the same time if you know what I mean." Sally giggled and said, "I know exactly what you mean. But you know

Tina; the first day is the worst of all. If you can make it through today, you'll have it made."

And in a painful voice Tina said, "I don't suppose I have any choice do I?" Sally frowned as she broke the news to Tina, "No dear. Mr. Ballard has already called for you and he wants to see you as soon as possible." Tina sighed with disgust when she said, "I was afraid of that. Give me five minutes and I'll hobble down to his office." Sally laughed and she disappeared from the room.

Just then Tina noticed her roses. They were beautiful and she leaned one over to smell it. The fragrance was heavenly and she smiled as she realized why she was putting her body through this torture.

So lovely, she thought. Then she dawned a stern and angry expression and said. "Look Mr. Samuel Morrison all this pain is your fault. I hope you're happy. I can hardly walk." She giggled realizing he had nothing to do with her pain. I don't even know the guy she thought. Because of his flowers she had made her decision to change her appearance, and for that, she was grateful. The flowers were only a reminder of why she was putting herself through this pain but it was the determination she had that made her feel strong and she knew that soon, very soon, she'd have that body she'd always dreamed of.

Each step was extremely painful but she slowly made her way to the scales and she held onto her desk for dear life in order to get there. That one small step, up to her scales, was painful, and she might as well have walked across the desert, she thought, and she snickered at her feebleness.

One thirty-five it said then she turned to glance at herself in the mirror. That's okay it won't be long now. She moved from the scales and she stumbled toward her desk to gather her things for the meeting with Mr. Ballard.

When she left her office she stopped to lean on Sally's desk to rest and gather her strength. Sally exclaimed, "Tina, are you going to make it?" Tina smiled, and a determined expression smothered her face as she said, "Not only will I make it but no one will even know I'm in any pain what so ever." Tina stood tall and she walked through the front door and down the hall as if there were no pain at all. Sally smiled and she admired Tina's spunk, and she watched her march through the door. What a tough lady she is, Sally thought, and Tina disappeared down the hall.

Tina smiled and she walked tall while she made her way toward Mr. Ballard's office. But with each step she took, she thought, Ouch, oh, ooh, but she continued, with a smile, and soon she stood in front of his door. She took a deep breath, renewed her determination, and entered his office. Mr. Ballard looked up as she did and asked, "Morning Tina you look radiant today have you met someone new?" Tina eased into the huge leather chair and she giggled before she replied, "No, Mr. Ballard. The only new thing that I've met lately is my new aerobics class."

"Well I must say it certainly agrees with you and you look wonderful." Tina blushed and she held her head to her shoulder and her legs ached, and her tummy, and her back, and her entire body, all the way down to her toes, but she held the pain in and she replied. "Thank you so much Mr. Ballard that means a lot to me."

Then, Mr. Ballard said, "I needed to see you early this morning because I have another appointment at nine-thirty, so let's get right to it. I finally received the results for the double burger combo promotion in Oklahoma, and they were much better than either of us had expected. Apparently, the new meat Ms. Cunningham, is trying to introduce, is a big hit. Sales, during the promotion were up 23% but even more dramatic than that, sales of her burger alone, were up 37% and still climbing. Apparently the customers love her product and I have to hand it to you for twisting my arm and persuading me to try it. Good job."

Tina was astounded, by the figures that Mr. Ballard was throwing at her, and she realized he felt as though they had stumbled across something great. She perked up, and came to life, and she put her pain behind her.

"Well thank you Mr. Ballard but you didn't need much persuading once you tasted her product for yourself." Mr. Ballard smiled as he said, "It was a very good burger and now I'd like for you to put together a proposal for us to run the same promotion throughout our company. I'll need projections, promotional costs, distribution of product, and an estimated date of execution for a nationwide promotion. And Tina, I want to move on this so let's shoot for Friday on the proposal if at all possible."

Her eyes lit up, realizing the magnitude of the project, and she loved it. She and Mr. Ballard had a tremendous respect for one another. They had successfully worked on many deals together but the confidence he showed in her, at this very moment, was the ultimate compliment. It excited her and her thoughts were filled with making this one a success too.

She sat straight up in her chair as she replied, "No problem, Mr. Ballard. I've been in constant contact with Ms. Cunningham and she's also eager to begin."

"Okay great," he said, as he stood and slowly began to pace the room as he spoke. "Now, concerning our conversation yesterday of the southern California marketing problems. Have you given it any further thought?"

She shook her head and shrugged her shoulders as she said, "Only that I feel our, Florida strategy, was a good one and it worked well for us." Mr. Ballard puffed on his cigar as he said, "Okay, I agree Tina." Then he held his index finger in front of his face as he said, "But, we'll only give it six months. If sales aren't up significantly, within that time frame, funds will be re-routed to the major markets. Is that agreeable with you?" Tina smiled and she replied, "Perfectly."

After discussing several other topics, the meeting was adjourned since Mr. Ballard had another appointment. Tina stood, with her aching and wobbly legs, but she held back the pain and she shook his hand and made her way toward the door.

Tina walked the halls with confidence now thinking how wonderful the meeting had been. Her pain and soreness were all but gone and she realized she had a mountain of work to accomplish by Friday. When she pushed the door open Sally had a surprised look on her face and she asked, "What happened? You look as though you just won the lottery?" Tina's excitement was on the verge of explosion as she replied, "Almost. The meeting was outstanding and if I can pull off this new promotion it'll be better than winning the lottery. Come into my office and I'll fill you in."

The power of Tina's enthusiasm was overwhelming and Sally anxiously followed her into the office. When Tina was seated Sally moved behind her, to read her notes along with her, and she placed her hands on Tina's shoulders. Tina could barely contain herself while she revealed her plan and Sally bent over to rest her chin on Tina's shoulder for a better look.

They were bubbling over with excitement, by the time Tina finished explaining, and Sally whispered into her ear, "I love you like this. You're a real turn on." Tina giggled as she said, "This whole deal is a real turn on." And she turned her head up to Sally, and Sally gave her a quick kiss to her lips.

Tina was startled by Sally's actions and she quickly stood from her chair and Sally said, "I'm sorry; I was caught up in the moment." Tina tried to shake it off and she didn't want to make a big deal out of it and she replied, "Don't worry about it I understand. Would you please get me the advertising folder for southern California?" Sally smiled and said, "I'd Love to," and she disappeared through the door to her filing cabinet.

Tina's thoughts ran wild while Sally was gone. She hadn't really understood Sally's actions and she was totally confused. She shook her head no, and she thought, I must have misunderstood, surely I did, but when Sally returned she was smiling from ear to ear and she had an unexpected bounce in her step and at that very instant Tina realized she hadn't misunderstood at all.

When Sally handed the folder to her Tina asked, "Sally, what's going on here?" Sally had a puzzled expression on her face. "What do you mean?"

For a moment Tina was at a loss. Her and Sally were very good friends and she didn't want to hurt Sally's feelings and what if she was wrong and had misunderstood? Maybe now was not the right time and she quickly said, "Oh, never mind. Will you get Ms. Cunningham on the line for me please?" Sally cheerfully replied, "Of course dear," and she left the office.

Tina was frustrated. Holly shit! She thought. Why didn't I say something? But she had so much work to do and this incident seemed so trivial she shrugged her shoulders and lost herself in work.

Before long Sally's voice could be heard through the intercom, "Tina, I have Ms. Cunningham on line one." "Thanks Sally."

"Hello Ms. Cunningham. How are you today?... I'm glad to hear that, I'm also doing just fine. Listen, Mr. Ballard and I met this morning concerning the results of the burger promotion in Oklahoma. The results are overwhelming.... I knew you'd be glad to hear that. Listen; before we make any decisions concerning a nationwide promotion you and I must hammer out the details of your producing and distributing 182,000 boxes of meat to each of our restaurants.... Fine. I'll need detailed reports from you outlining the routing, delivery dates, and a projection of any anticipated problems.... Yes Ms. Cunningham but we need an alternate plan in case there's a problem somewhere down the line.... Yes, yes of course, but we'll be spending millions advertising this promotion and we need to see a backup plan. Mr. Ballard and I will meet on this subject again Friday so I need your information by Thursday. Simply fax the information to me Thursday morning. You do have our fax number don't you?... Okay fine I'll be waiting to hear from you Thursday. Bye-bye."

A smile of success ran across Tina's face and she let out a sigh of relief as she called Sally. "Sally, please get me Mr. Barnes, from Multi-Media Advertising." "Right away," replied Sally.

Tina sat back in her chair and she contemplated her conversation with Mr. Barnes. He's the producer of Burgers Inc. television commercials and he's done quite well for our company the past four years she thought. I hope he's got at least one more great idea up his sleeve!

Before long Sally's voice interrupted Tina's thoughts. "I have Mr. Barnes on line three, and your mom on line two. Your mom says she's going to be out of pocket and she needs to speak with you briefly." As Tina picked up on line two, she said, "Ok, thanks Sally. Hello mom. Listen. I'm sorry but I have a very critical call waiting on another line.... Yes, mom I know its dad's birthday next month.... You're going to buy him a boat?... Mom that's a bit extravagant don't you think?... Okay I think gray would be a good color. Okay. Bye mom. I've got to run; I'll call you later okay? Great, bye mom. I love you too."

Then Tina picked up line three and said, "Hello, Mr. Barnes sorry for the delay. Burgers Inc. is planning a huge promotion for the entire month of July. It's a nationwide promotion and we need for you to dig deep inside yourself and create something extra special for us.... I see, you can't have it that soon. Well, Mr. Barnes July is what we're shooting for. Mr. Ballard wants to get this one off the ground as soon as possible.... Okay check your schedule, with that in mind, and call me right back. Thank you. Bye now."

Damn it, she thought, as she hung up the phone. There has got to be a way! We've simply got to run this promotion in July. She was deep in thought when Sally walked in. When Sally saw the tension on Tina's face she laid some papers on Tina's desk and she slithered behind her chair and she began massaging her shoulders.

"How's your pain?" she asked, as Tina sat back to enjoy the massage. "What pain? Tina asked and then she continued, oh the aerobics pain." Tina realized she hadn't even noticed the pain and she said, "It's not completely gone but that feels sooo.... good... don't stop." Then Tina closed her eyes in sheer pleasure and she said, "Please don't stop..... Oh Sally you missed your calling." Sally smiled and she moved Tina's hair aside and she began massaging her neck. When Tina was totally relaxed Sally stopped and she rested her hands on Tina's shoulders and Tina reached her hands up to Sally's and she pressed them flat against her shoulders. Then she patted them as she said, "Thanks darling that's just what I needed."

Just then the phone rang and Sally made a move for it but Tina waved her hand as if to say, that's okay I'll get it. Sally stood with her hands flat on Tina's shoulders and Tina answered the phone. "Burgers Inc. may I help you? Oh hi mom. No I'm not busy now."

Sally began rubbing her hands back and forth on Tina's shoulders in a caressing sort of way while Tina spoke on the phone. "No Sally's right here so I answered for her." Tina giggled as she reached up with one hand and she patted one of Sally's.

"Hold on mom let me get my pencil." While she reached for her pencil Sally slid her hands down the front of Tina's blouse and then back up in a slow caressing motion. Tina was caught up in her conversation with her mom and she didn't pay much attention. "Okay mom, go ahead...." While Tina was writing Sally slid her hands down the front of Tina's blouse one more time. This time touching Tina's breasts and Sally dragged her fingertips slowly across the nipples several times and then she moved her hands back to Tina's shoulders. "No mom, I... I'm okay, I was in Sally's way and I had to move."…. Then she stared up at Sally, with a puzzled expression on her face, then back down to her notes.

For the third time Sally slid her hands down the front of Tina's blouse. This time Sally cupped her hands and she slowly moved them to the sides of Tina's breasts and she took them into her hands. Tina dropped her pencil and she raised her free hand to stop Sally's hands right where they were but Joan asked Tina a question and she had to answer, "Yes mom I know where that is...." Tina patted Sally's hands and she reached for her pencil. Sally gave Tina's breasts a little squeeze and she slowly but intimately dragged her fingertips alongside them and she brought her hands back to Tina's shoulders.

Acting as though she wanted to leave the room, before Tina ended her conversation, Sally patted Tina's shoulders and she began to slowly ease out of sight. Tina watched Sally seductively; move across the room and out the door. "Okay mom I'll be there at eleven-thirty. Bye-bye mom."

Tina's face was flush when she hung up the phone. She was hot and she took a deep breath and her heart was throbbing. She raised her hand to her breast and her nipples were hard. What just happened here she thought? I can't believe it. She stood and she began to pace. What has gotten into Sally, she thought? In the year and a half, I've known that woman; she has never touched me in such a way. Sure we've called each other honey, dear, sweetheart, and other loving names but we've never touched. At least not like that.

Tina tried to shake those thoughts from her mind and then she heard Sally's voice on the intercom, "Tina, its Mr. Barnes on line two." Very surprised to hear from Mr. Barnes this quickly Tina said, "Oh, thank you Sally."

She reached over to pick up her phone, "Hello, Mr. Barnes, this is Tina..... I'm so glad to hear you may be able to work this in...... Yes, it's the double burger combo. The meat on the burger will be a new product for us so we need a very explosive spot..... Mr. Barnes I appreciate it very much and I'll be waiting for your call tomorrow, to confirm, you're being able to complete this project by June...... Thank you Mr. Barnes you've made my day. Bye-bye.

Tina was over joyed when she hung up the phone and her thoughts were lost in the excitement and she had all but forgotten Sally's apparent advances. "Sally, may I see you for a moment please." Tina stood, and she began to straighten the files which Sally had brought in earlier. When Sally entered Tina was bubbling with excitement because of the news Mr. Barnes had for her. "All's well with the new promotion, she said, and then she continued, "I only need for everyone to come through for me now."

Sally quickly made her way to Tina's side and they hugged with excitement. Tina smiled from ear to ear as she said, "I have to break for lunch now. I've got to meet mom at Whitney boats. She's buying dad a new boat for his birthday next month and she wants me to help her pick it out."

Tina was excited about her entire day and she couldn't be still and Sally said, "If you go now you won't need to drive you could just float." They both laughed and Tina made her way toward the door and then she turned toward Sally and asked, "It's that obvious, huh?" Sally replied, "Yeah I'm afraid so." Tina smiled and said, "By the way here's the southern California file folder I'll be back by two o'clock," suddenly, she was gone.

When Tina arrived at Whitney's she didn't see Joan, at first, and she checked her clock to find it was only eleven-twenty-seven. Surely she's here, Tina thought, while she parked her car. Then as she opened the car door and slid out she saw Joan coming out the front door. Joan had the expression of a child on Christmas day spread across her face and her eyes were opened wide and her inquisitive looking smile was a dead giveaway. She was having the time of her life.

When Tina approached Joan she couldn't help but giggle. Joan was such a sight, and she snatched Tina's hand and she began pulling her inside. "Oh dear I've found the most perfect boat for your father. Just wait till you see it." While Tina tried to slow her down she remarked, "Mom, give me a break we'll get there soon enough." And she giggled at her mom's excitement.

Tina was in awe when she saw the boat Joan had picked out for James. "Oh mom what is daddy going to do with a boat that large?" Joan said, "Well honey, he can fish, and ski, and we can throw parties...and..." Tina laughed out loud as she said, "Mom this is outrageous. It's more like a house than a boat."

Just then a smiling salesman eased his way toward them but he looked as though he was moving in for the kill as he said, "Hi ladies. She's beautiful isn't she?" Tina held her hand flat to her chest as she looked the boat over. "It certainly is how much for this little baby?" "Only $120,000, he replied." Tina almost fell out and she grabbed Joan's arm and she began to pull her away. "Come on mom let's look around." They left the salesman standing alone and Tina snuggled next to Joan and said, "Mom get real. Let's be practical. Daddy doesn't like to ski and you have plenty of parties at home. So what does he really need?"

Joan looked as though someone had just let the air out of her balloon as she said, "I know dear but I want this to be a special gift." Tina realized she had hurt Joan's feelings and she hugged her neck and said, "Mom, I'm sorry for being so practical if you want to buy that boat for him let's go, the salesman is still waiting." They glanced at the $120,000 boat and the salesman was wiping it down. Joan's expression suddenly changed and her face lit up once again, "Na," she said. "Here's another boat I looked at earlier. It's a cute little Ranger bass boat." Once again, Tina giggled, when Joan became carried away.

Joan's excitement began to get the best of her and she walked to the back of the boat and said, "See here's the little motor." Then she giggled and walked toward the front of the boat and she said, "And here's the little seat, and steering wheel, and up front here, is a teeny tiny motor, for emergencies, I guess." "No mom!" Tina said in a playful sort of way. "That's called a trolling motor. It's for slow fishing."

Tina stared Joan in the eyes and asked, "Well, what do you think mom?" "I love it" Joan said, "But, do you think he will?" Tina smiled and said, "Mom, he'll love it. It's beautiful."

Tina signaled for the salesman to come over and he smiled again and with that vulture-like expression he casually strolled to their sides. "Yes ma'am. Have we made a decision?" Tina dawned an odd expression on her face as she said, "Yes we have." And Tina frowned at him, not liking his attitude. Tina pointed at a sign as she said, "The sign on this boat says its $22,000. Then it says speak with a salesperson first! What does that mean?"

Tina didn't like this salesman. His attitude was cocky and arrogant and he smiled and leaned against the boat as she listened to his answer. "It means, it's your lucky day," he said and with a sneaky sort of smile he said, "Today it's only $20,795. "Oh no" Tina said, "That's far too much for this little boat." The salesman quickly replied, "But ma'am, it's a sixteen-foot bass boat and for a bass boat that is not small at all." Then he said, "I promise you, that price is as low as you'll find anywhere."

Joan became nervous while she watched Tina handle the salesman. Joan had seen Tina in action before but she sensed that Tina didn't care for this man at all and she knew that there would be a real battle over the price. Joan also knew that Tina would win, as usual.

Tina walked around the boat and she gave it, the once over, "No I think not that's more than we wanted to spend." She grabbed Joan's hand again, and she began to lead her away as Tina said, "We'll go to Bill's boating center across the street and do some price shopping and Tina said, "Come on mom." "Hold on just a second," he shouted. The girls stopped and they turned toward the salesman and he said, "Before you go to Bill's let me talk to my manager. I may be able to do a little better on that price. Will that be okay?"

Tina glanced at Joan and she shrugged her shoulders as if to question Joan. Then Tina turned toward the salesman and said, "Okay but we're on our lunch hour and I don't have all day." The salesman held his index finger to his face as he said, "one moment. I'll be right back," and he turned and hustled away.

Tina and Joan joined hands and they laughed out loud. Joan was laughing hard and she said, "Tina you are just like your father.... you are too much! What price do you think he will come back with?" Tina shrugged her shoulders and said, "I don't know mom but whatever it is he's gonna take less. "They laughed again and Joan walked next to the boat and she touched it as she asked, "Do you really think he'll like it?" Tina closed her eyes and exhaled as she moved to Joan's side and she gave Joan a little hug as she said, "Yes mom, he's gonna love it. I promise."

Before long the salesman returned and with a glum expression on his face and he stated, "I'm sorry ladies but the manager informed me the price has already been lowered to rock bottom. However, he did allow me to round it down to $20,500." Tina shook her head no and said, "That will never do we'll give you $20,000 and not a penny more!" Then Tina took her mom's arm and led her toward the front door.

The salesman looked nervous, and worried, and he even began perspiring a bit. He rested his hands behind his back, and he paced back and forth for a moment. Finally, he stopped his pacing and he turned toward the girls and he said, "Okay. I'll probably lose my job over this but if you buy right now, today, I'll let you have it for $20,000."

A smile of victory ran across Tina and Joan's faces and they stared each other in the eyes and they joined hands as Tina asked, "well mom how about it?" Joan jumped for joy as she said, "Let's do it." Tina turned toward the salesman and said with confidence, "SOLD!" The salesman began breathing again as he said, "Great, follow me and we'll fill out the papers. Joan interrupted, "Excuse me. Would it be possible for you to store this boat for us for forty days?" "Forty days?" he asked. Tina quickly jumped in to say, "You see it's a birthday gift for my daddy and his birthday is in forty days."

"That's a bit unusual," he responded, "Just a moment, I'll check with the manager." While he was gone Tina and Joan checked the boat out thoroughly. Tina knew a little bit about bass boats but Joan knew nothing. Tina felt proud that her mother had confidence in her and that she had asked her for help. Tina was proud that they were able to negotiate a good deal. But most of all she was proud of her mother for wanting to make this birthday a special one for James. Tina could imagine the expression on James' face when Joan presents it to him, on his birthday, and she felt warm inside just thinking about it, and she smiled.

Before they knew it the salesman returned with a smile this time, and he said "The manager informed me there would be a fifty-dollar charge for that length of time." Tina looked at Joan and said, "Mom, if the boat is stored here you won't have to insure it until we take it home that should cover the fifty dollars. What do you think?" Joan nodded, okay, and Tina turned toward the salesman again and she replied, "Ok, that will be fine let's sign those papers I've got to go."

When they reached the manager's office Tina turned to face Joan and she asked, "Mom, its twelve-thirty and I've got to get back to work will you be okay?" Joan said, "Well of course dear I appreciate your help?" Joan leaned toward Tina and she kissed her cheek as she said, "I love you baby. Thanks." Tina looked Joan in the eyes and replied, "I love you too mom, I'll call you later ok? Bye now." Joan smiled and she gave Tina a little wave and she said, "Bye dear."

She left Whitney's with a good feeling and she imagined her daddy's surprise on his birthday. She smiled as thoughts of her mom's excitement drifted through her mind and she even giggled out loud at times from those thoughts. They're damned good people she thought. The best.

Suddenly a rush of fantasies filled Tina's mind, while she drove down the highway. Once again she pictured Mr. Morrison seated at a restaurant table waiting for her arrival. Tina was elegant in her satin, low cut dress, and as she approached Samuel all eyes were focused on her. She was slim and very tempting and

Samuel rose to his feet and he took her hand in his and he very gently kissed it.

She sat directly across from him and they laughed the dinner hour away then they retired to his suite. When he opened the door, Tina imagined, the furniture was white and a fire was roaring in the fireplace. Samuel gently took her coat and then he turned her around for a soft kiss before he laid her coat on the chair. She heard Samuel's voice say, "Make yourself at home," while he poured Champaign and then he made his way to her side, in front of the fireplace, where they toasted one another. Then Samuel gathered both glasses and sits them on a nearby table and he returned to Tina's arms for the kiss of a lifetime.

Tina was suddenly brought back to reality by the honking of someone's horn. Damn it she thought. That's the story of my life. Just when it's about to happen....! She thought. And she maneuvered her car to the far right lane thinking she would be left alone where the traffic was slower. Then thoughts of Sally entered her mind.

Tina glanced at her face in the rear view mirror as she wondered about Sally. What's going on with that girl? She wondered. Then she remembered the feeling of Sally holding her breasts in the palm of her hands this morning and Tina's nipples began to harden just thinking of it.

Tina smiled as she thought how good it felt for someone, anyone, to touch her. It's been awhile, she thought, and thinking of Sally touching her was extremely exciting, almost explosive. At that moment Tina realized that she would have to have a chat with Sally immediately and put a stop to her actions. "As much as I love Sally, this cannot go any further than it already has.

When she walked through the doors of Burgers Inc., Sally was on the phone and Tina smiled and she wiggled her fingers at Sally, as if to say hi, and she made her way toward her office.

Once inside she sat down and she realized how glad she was that Sally was on the phone when she entered the room. That sure made it easier for me, she thought. Then Tina became angry and she slammed her fist on her desk. "Damn you Sally I love you too much for this!"

CHAPTER 4

The Trials of Friendship

The afternoon crept by for Tina, and while she tried to complete her work, thoughts of Sally, drifted in and out of her mind. Something had to be done, and something had to be done soon. But what, she thought? Finally, she decided, Sally had to be confronted. While she stared at the wall in front of her, a stern, determined expression appeared on her face, and she imagined the conversation they might have. Before long, she nodded her head yes, and she thought, I'll do it!

She glanced at the clock, and it was five o'clock. No better time than the present, she thought then she called, "Sally, could I see you for a moment please?" Tina heard Sally's voice as she said, "I'll be right there Tina." While she waited for Sally, her thoughts ran wild. I certainly don't want to hurt her feelings, but I can't be her lover either. Oh well, it'll all work out, I hope.

Sally seemed a little tired, when she entered Tina's office, but even at her worst, she still looked delicious. I hope I'm not sorry for this later, Tina thought

Tina seemed a little taken back as she saw Sally and she said, "You look worn out Sally." Sally found renewed energy, as she smiled and said, "No, I'm fine. Really. You know how it is to answer the phone all day. There's a lot of irritating people in the world." Tina giggled and said, "You can say that again."

Then, Tina's expression shifted to one of seriousness. "Sally, I have a little problem, and I need your help and understanding with it." Sally gritted her teeth, and dawned an odd expression, as if she had done something wrong, and she was waiting for the boom to be lowered. Tina nervously stood, and she took Sally's hand, and they moved to the sofa, and had a seat.
Sally had a very puzzled expression on her face, as she remarked, "This seems a little serious." Tina answered, "I certainly hope not." Sally leaned toward Tina in anticipation, not wanting to miss a word. Tina smiled, and stared directly into Sally's eyes. "Sally.... you and I have been through many things together, huh? And I consider you a very, very close friend." Sally nodded, as if to say, yeah, so what. Then Tina patted Sally's hand as she said, "And I would never, do anything to change, or harm our relationship, you know that don't you?" Sally raised her eye brows, and nodded yes.

Tina continued, "Well. . . . This is difficult for me. . . .But today, something took place. . . . Something I don't understand." Tina squeezed Sally's hand, and she was having difficulty saying the words. Tina paused, and she tried to regroup, then she stood, and began pacing the floor.

Then, she said, "Goddamn it! Why is this so difficult? I can speak just fine to any chairman, of any board of directors in this country, but I'll be damned if I can talk to you about this. Sally, I only know one way to say this." Tina reseated herself next to Sally, and she took her hand again.

Tina became teary eyed, as she blurted out. "Sally.. .. Today you kissed my lips, and you held my breasts in your hands, and I don't understand."

Sally pulled her hand from Tina's, and she lowered her head in shame. She began slowly shaking her head no, and she cried, and she brought her hands to her face. In a very soft voice, she replied, "I'm sorry Tina, I couldn't help myself."

Tina reached her hand to Sally, and she brushed the hair from Sally's face and said "Sally, I only want to understand."

Sally removed her hands from her face, but she looked away from Tina, and in a broken voice she said, "Tina. . . . You're so damned exciting to me."

Tina quickly asked, "Sally, what do you mean?" Sally took a deep breath, and she tried to stop the tears, but she couldn't. Tina reached toward her desk, for the box of tissues, and she handed it to Sally, and Sally took one, and she laid the box on the sofa between them, and she dried her eyes.

Tina realized that Sally wasn't going to answer any time soon, and she asked her another question.

"Sally. You and I have double dated in the past, and I've seen you with many men. I've even seen you kiss a man, and I've seen how you held him, and touched him. . . .And, I simply can't believe that you're. . . gay!"

Sally, quickly turned toward Tina, and she sat up straight, and had an angry expression on her face as she said, "I am not gay!"

Tina asked, "Well then, what are you saying Sally?" Sally relaxed, and slumped into the sofa, as if to resign. She wiped her tears once again, and she turned to face Tina and she said, "Tina, sometimes.... I love to be touched by a woman. I love to be held by a woman. And yes, I love to kiss a woman, but I am not gay! Occasionally, I do want a woman next to me, even more than I want a man. Can you possibly understand?"

Tina shook her head as she said, "No I can't Sally, help me! Please, help me!"

Sally said, "I can't explain it any better than that. I would never want a permanent relationship with a woman, but I do adore being with one, occasionally."

In shock, from what Sally had said, Tina asked, "Sally, how many women have you been with…?" Then Sally interrupted, "Tina, don't be so nosy!" Tina said, "I'm not being nosy. I'm trying to understand." Sally had tears streaming down her cheeks, and she thought for a moment, then she scanned Tina's body as she said, "Only one." Tina blurted out, "Only one? And how many times were you with her?" Sally glared at Tina, as if to say, how dare you ask these questions and then Sally said, "Twice."

Tina asked, "Let me get this straight, you've been with one woman, on two separate occasions, and I assume you made love to her?" Sally closed her eyes for a second, and she took in a deep breath and said, "Actually, she made love to me." Tina quickly stood, and screamed, "What difference does it make, you had sex with a woman, is that right!" In defense, Sally stood as she pleaded with Tina to understand. "Tina, what is your problem? You act as though you're jealous."

Tina gathered herself for a moment, and then she sat next to Sally again, and Tina took Sally's hand and said, "Look Sally, I'm sorry. I didn't mean to raise my voice, but don't be silly, I'm not jealous. I...I guess I'm curious. If anyone had told me yesterday, that I'd be sitting here talking to anyone on this subject, I would have laughed." Sally quickly said, "Oh believe me, I understand. I never would've believed, a couple of months ago, that I would feel this way either." Tina sighed, shrugged her shoulders and said, "Boy, what a day." Sally snickered and said, "Really."

Then Tina sat back on the soft and asked, "Sally, how did all this start?" Sally took a deep breath as she said, "Innocently." Then, she stared into Tina's eyes and asked, "Do you remember how it started for us, today?" Tina jumped up, from her seat once again, and she glared at Sally and she yelled, "Wait a minute Sally. Nothing started for us today!" Sally became nervous, and she realized she had said the wrong thing, and then she tried to smooth it over by saying, "I'm sorry. I know that."

Then Sally continued, "Look Tina, a couple of months ago, I was at a dear friends house. A lady I have known for ten years, or more. I was in her kitchen making a pitcher of iced tea, and she came up behind me, and rested her hand on my back, and we began to talk, about something, I don't remember what.

Before long, her hand began to wander." Sally shrugged her shoulders as she continued, "And.... and we ended up in each other's arms. I don't know, it just happened."

"And?" Tina asked with a curious twinkle in her eye. Then Sally continued, "And, we ended up in bed together."

Tina had only heard of such things, but did not personally know a woman, who had made love to another. But she could almost understand, especially after the thoughts she had earlier, of her and Sally. It became exciting to talk about this subject, and she had an anxious expression on her face, as she stared deeply into Sally's eyes, and Tina wanted to hear more.

Then she asked, "What about the second time?" Sally wiped her eyes, and said, "She called me one night, about a week later, and said she was lonely. She asked me if I would stop by, and have a drink. To be honest. . . . I thought about her almost every day, after that first time." Sally almost seemed as though she were trying to convince Tina that this relationship was not a bad thing, then she continued, "Tina, it was so good! At first, I felt just like you do now. But afterwards, I couldn't get her off my mind, and I became obsessed with it, if that makes any since."

"After that second time, Sally continued, she moved away. I went to her house, after work one afternoon, and she was gone. There was no note, no message, no nothing, she simply vanished. That was three weeks ago. Then today, you were so excited about your success. . .

And I simply got caught up in it, and it seemed right to me. Tina, I'm so sorry. I really am." Sally buried her face into her hands, and she began crying.

Tina stopped pacing, and she smiled at Sally, and she sat next to her, and held her hand again and said, "Sally thanks for sharing that with me." She lifted her hand to Sally's chin, and she raised it so she could gaze into Sally's eyes and said, "Look, I'm sorry your friend moved away, but.... Sally?.... I can't. . . .I simply can't be your lover." Sally squeezed Tina's hand, and she sniffled, and then she giggled as she said, "Tina, I'm so sorry. Yes, I'm attracted to you, and yes you're a turn on for me, but I never intended to offend you. Tina, I promise you, here and now, you have absolutely nothing to worry about."

Tina's expression, turned to one of forgiveness, and she held Sally's chin in her hand, and she said. "I think the world of you Sally, you're a very special lady, but what you've just told me is all new to me, and I don't really know what to think." Then Tina paused as she said, "But I will say this, I do understand how you feel." Then she nodded to Sally as she said, "I really do."

Sally took a breath, and she wiped her tears, and she became relieved as she said, "Tina, I'm glad you're not angry, and I promise, I'll never touch you again."

Tina, took Sally's hand in hers, and giggled. "Sally, touching is fine; you know I'm a toucher. It's the type of touching that made me uncomfortable. Okay?"

Sally smiled from ear to ear, and she squeezed Tina's hand, and nodded yes as she said, "Thanks Tina."

Sally stood, and they hugged and then they wiped each other's tears, and then she leaned back, and she stared into Tina's eyes and asked, "See you tomorrow?" Tina nodded yes, and smiled as she answered, "I still love you Sally. I hope you know that." Sally gently closed her eyes for a moment, and smiled while she said, "That means everything to me Tina Thanks again," and Sally kissed Tina's cheek, and she disappeared through the door.

Once Sally left the office, Tina sat alone for a few moments, and tried to sort out her   feelings. The events of the day had been unbelievable. Not only had Tina been kissed and caressed by Sally, but Tina also experienced a fantasy which involved Sally. Tina had been told the most unbelievable story, one of her best friend making it with another woman, and Tina was suddenly envious of Sally's boldness, and the freedom she seemed to possess. Then there was Sally's accusation of Tina being jealous, and Tina smiled from that thought, and silently admitted to herself, she actually had been jealous. There was Sally's admission that **Tina** was a turn on to her, and that she was attracted to Tina. The thought of another woman being attracted to her, in any sexual sense, was exciting, and new, and different, and as Tina visualized Sally's beautiful face, in her mind, she could certainly understand how Sally's heart must have been broken when her friend disappeared, without a word.

Tina realized how easily she could be drawn into this new and exciting world of women being intimate with other women. She remembered the feeling of Sally's warm and soft hands, as they slid down the front of her blouse, and the sensational feeling she had, as Sally's fingers dragged across her nipples. Suddenly,

Tina realized, that as Sally was caressing her, and holding her breasts in her hands, and fondling her, that she could have stopped Sally at any time, but for some unknown reason, she didn't. That thought seemed to finally reach the core of Tina's dilemma. Why didn't she stop Sally?

Tina had no reason for not stopping Sally. But she smiled as she realized the tremendous pleasure and excitement that Sally had given her today, and for that, Tina was thankful.

CHAPTER 5

The Joy of Success

Forty-eight, forty-nine, fifty, Tina counted, as she finished her last rep of sit-ups. The past four weeks have been tough, she thought, as she stood, and grabbed her towel, but one of the best achievements of my life. She was beside herself, as she realized how close she was to achieving her goal, and she hurried to the dressing room to look into the full length mirror. She smiled endlessly, as she thought, you're almost there baby.

Her breasts were firm, and her entire body was sleek and trim. She had an expression of approval on her face, while she stared with pride. Only one little spot left, she thought, and she turned sideways, and she patted her small, but slightly protruding tummy. When this is gone, I'll finally have that perfect body, I've always dreamed of. Move over Sally, Tina is coming through, she playfully thought, and then she made her way toward her locker.

While Tina dressed, she hummed a cheerful little tune, and she glanced at the clock to find it was only eight-twenty p.m., and as she thought of how she might spend the remainder of the evening. It suddenly hit her, that she needed a new wardrobe for her new sensual, sexual, and slim body. I've never been able to buy revealing clothing, she thought, I might need some help, and instantly, Sally came to mind. That's it, she exclaimed, Sally is the hottest dresser I know. That woman knows how to pick, and fit clothing to flow just perfectly, around each curve of a woman's body.

With that thought in mind, Tina's smile attracted all sorts of attention, when she walked past the front desk, and through the front doors of Sterling's, and to her car. She carried herself with great confidence, while she thought of the sexy clothing, Sally may pick out, for her to wear to Boston next week.

When she drove from Sterling's, her mind was filled with thoughts of all the last minute details to be done before her trip. Let's see, she thought, if I can talk Sally into helping me with my new wardrobe tomorrow, I'll have something sensual to wear, when Bob takes me out for my bon voyage party. Boy will he be surprised, she thought, as she turned into her driveway at home. After she unlocked her front door, she swiftly walked to her bedroom, and she ripped her clothing off, and fell into her bed, and she picked up the phone, to call Sally. I hope she's home, she thought, as she dialed the number.

When Sally answered, Tina used a soft sexual voice, and said, "Hello darling. My beautiful new body aches for a man. Do you know of any, off hand?" Tina giggled. "I'm only kidding Sally. I'm actually saving myself, for Mr. Right!" and she giggled again. "No seriously, do you have any   plans for lunch tomorrow? Great, I was wondering if you might help me pick out a new, sexy wardrobe tomorrow. You know, one that'll knock their socks off, in Boston. Well, in Dallas too, for that matter."

Tina blurted out, "Money is no object. Only the best for this gorgeous body, and of course, we'll have to pay Victoria a visit for some very comfortable and hot sleepware, if you know what I mean. I wouldn't want to have any sleepless nights in Boston you know," and Tina roared with laughter. "Okay dear, I'll see you in the morning, bye-bye."

After she laid the phone down, she held her hand on it, for a moment, and she stared into space, imagining the hot and tantalizing outfits that Sally would select for her. As those thoughts ran through her mind, she slowly stood, and walked into the bathroom, almost in a trance, and she started her shower. Then she walked back into her bedroom, and she turned every light on, and stood in front of her mirror. A strange sensation ran through her body, and she couldn't help herself. She had the urge to feel this new body. She ran her hands down the sides of her sleek curves, and she smiled with pride as she thought, you are gorgeous and I am so proud of you.

Tina had a seat on the edge of her bed as thoughts of her trip to Boston flooded her mind. It's only for a few days, she thought, and then I will be back home. Then she thought of her flowers and Mr. Samuel Morrison and she fantasied, maybe I will just decide to move to Boston, and she giggled.

Suddenly, Tina came back to reality, and she realized the shower was still running. She quickly jumped up, and ran to it, but no damage was done. She sighed with relief, and eased herself into the shower. When the water splashed against her body, the feeling was incredible and she leaned against the wall, and smiled thinking of that Morrison guy.

After Tina turned the water off, and dried her gorgeous body, she fell into her bed, and relaxed. Suddenly, the phone rang so loud, it almost shook her from the bed. Not wanting to hear that dreaded ring again, she quickly snatched the receiver to her ear.

"Hello? She asked. "Oh, hello Bob," and she giggled. "No, I wasn't setting on the phone silly; the ring startled me, so I answered it quickly. Oh, I'm just lying here, in bed, thinking about Boston. No, I don't have any clothes on," she giggled. "Why?" Tina became excited, and she began to stroke her nipples, and soon her hand was rubbing her tummy, while she spoke. "You silly thing, what makes you think I was thinking of you? Well, I may have. I guess you'll never know," and she laughed. "Actually, I just got out of the shower, and I haven't had a chance to dress yet."

"Yes Darling, I'm soaking wet," she said, with a very soft and seductive tone. "Oh honey, I wish you were here to dry my back too. I can't quite reach it all by myself, and ooh, it would feel so good."

Just at that moment, she giggled at Bob. "Well darling, this is my late night voice, do you like it? She began laughing, and asked, "Are you still there? Then, she listened to Bob tell her, he only called to say good night. "Oh Bob, you're so sweet. Thanks, and I hope you sleep well too. Bye dear. Sweet dreams. I love ya."

As Tina hung the phone up she felt warm and snuggly, while she laid there smiling from ear to ear. Then she thought. That Bob has been my rock for many years and I love that guy.

It was still early, only ten o'clock, and she decided to treat herself to a glass of wine. It felt wonderful, after her shower and that beautiful conversation with Bob. She smiled and closed her eyes, while she enjoyed every twinge she had, then she grabbed her robe, and slowly made her way to the kitchen, where she poured herself a glass of wine. She took a sip, and noticed the moonlight shining through her patio window, and she walked over, and slid the glass door open, then she eased over to a padded chair, and had a seat.

She stared at the moon, and smiled, and she took another sip of wine, and she thought of her parents. Her mom had been so charming while picking out James' boat for his birthday, and she could almost picture her face in her mind, and she giggled. Tina had another sip of wine, and she placed her glass on the table in front of her. The night air sent a chill down her spine, so she lifted her feet to the chair, and she wrapped her arms around herself, and happy thoughts, filled her mind, and before long, she drifted off to sleep.

CHAPTER 6

Shopping For a New Body

The sun was bright, and Tina was awakened by the sound of singing birds, then she giggled, realizing she had fallen asleep on the patio last night. How silly, she thought, then the sight of two sparrows chasing one another from tree to tree caught her eye, and she smiled, while she watched. Tina began to remember those wonderful feelings of last night, and somehow, in the sunlight, she felt a little guilt ridden. But she quickly discounted it, and she realized that no one knew about last night, except for her, and that thought made her smile. Life is wonderful, she thought, and then she stood, and stretched, as if she were reaching for the sky. She looked like Rocky Balboa, standing in the morning light, reaching for victory.

Tina picked up her empty wine glass, and she headed for the kitchen for some fresh brewed coffee. While she leaned against the counter and watched the coffee brew, she realized she hadn't slept that well in months. That outdoor life must agree with me, she thought, but I wish this coffee would hurry up, I need my caffeine.

Once Tina was dressed, and ready for work, she made her way to the front door, and she began to smile, when she realized that her and Sally were going shopping during lunch today. I can't wait to see what that sexy little woman picks out for me, she thought. I'll be one hot woman when she gets finished with me. Before Tina left for work, she checked her wallet, and made sure she had her credit cards. She smiled from ear to ear, thinking, there's over four thousand dollars left on this one, that should do it, and she giggled, as she bounced outside to her car, and made her way to work

.

When Tina arrived at work, she was thinking how great of a day it was, and then she looked over to find Mr. Watkins greeting people, while they entered the building. He's been on vacation for two weeks now, and this will be his first glance at my hot, new body, she thought. He was stunned, while he watched her slither toward him. Tina giggled, and said, "Mr. Watkins, you'd better close your mouth, something might fly into it." He placed his hand on his forehead as he said, "Tina, you're.... why you're gorgeous." He smiled, from surprise, and he took her hand as he said, "Turn around, and let me look at you. My-my, you are absolutely beautiful." Tina smiled, as she replied, "Thanks Mr. Watkins. See what happens when you take a vacation, everyone changes, while you're gone, don't they?" He nodded yes and said, "I suppose they do dear, then he stood back and held his arms out as he said, but look at me, I haven't changed a bit." Tina giggled and smiled as she said, "Mr. Watkins, why would you want to change? You're perfect the way you are." He blushed as he said, "You're being kind, but thank you Tina."

She wiggled her new little butt, as she disappeared toward the elevators. She felt like a new woman, and she wanted to show it off a bit. While she stood, in the crowd, waiting for an elevator, Malcomb snuck up behind her, and he placed his hand breast high, on her side, and he ran it down to her hip. Surprised, Tina jumped, and quickly turned to find him laughing up a storm. Tina found that stern, Malcomb expression, as she said, "All right Malcomb, if I knew karate, you'd be hurting now."

Then Malcomb responded, "Tina, Tina, Tina, I'm so proud of you. You look fabulous, and you feel, uh-la-la." Tina blushed and asked, "Do you really think so?" Malcomb sealed his lips, and he nodded yes. Just then the elevator doors opened. Tina said, "Thanks Malcomb, but you know, the best part is, I feel great too!" Then Malcomb said, "I already said that Tina." Then Malcomb laughed. Tina playfully hit Malcomb on the shoulder and she said, "I mean inside silly." "Oh well, he said, here, let me touch the outside again." He reached out, as if to get a handful of her, and she ran inside the elevator, in order to escape him. Once he entered the elevator, Tina slapped his hand, and Malcomb grabbed it, as if he was wounded, then he said, "Ouch, you never minded me doing that before." Tina stood proud as she said, "Well, this is the new me. I'm saving myself for Mr. Right. No touching!"

They both laughed, and the door closed, and the elevator began moving. Malcomb said, "You're going to Boston next week aren't you?" Tina fixed a halfhearted smiled on her face, and replied, "Yeah, Monday." He said, "I'll bet you're excited, aren't you?" Tina's smile disappeared, and she slowly shook her head no. "No?" he asked. Tina watched the elevator numbers appear above the door, 5... 6...7... and she had a sad tone in her voice as she said; "I don't enjoy long business trips. They're dull and boring, and I don't know anyone there." 9...10...11... Then he said, "Yeah, but baby, you've got to get out and explore. There's so much to do in Boston." Tina asked, "Yeah, like what?" Malcomb said, "Well, there's the Red Sox."---Tina quickly interrupted and said, "OH Malcomb, that's just like you. Who but you, would think of the Red Sox?" 12...14. Then Tina broke the silence as she said, "Malcomb, it's been nice." Then Tina pointed to the doors, as they opened and she stepped outside, she said, "Bye-bye Malcomb." With a sheepish expression on his face, he waved and said, "Bye Tina."

She turned, and pushed the door of Burgers Inc. open, and as she did, she could see Sally, bent over reaching for a file, out of the second drawer of the filing cabinet. Tina just stood there in awe, and watched her for a moment. Sally's short cotton dress caressed her perfectly shaped butt, and Tina's eyes followed Sally's hose, as they disappeared underneath it. She couldn't believe the feelings and thoughts that she was having. Tina suddenly realized that never before, had she paid so much attention to another women's body. She couldn't help herself, and she almost felt lust for Sally, and she became embarrassed, but she quickly returned to a feeling of passion. Tina thought, if I were a man, I'd have a ....well. . . . And finally, she strolled into the office and said, "Honey, you'd better watch that bending over stuff, if you know what I mean."

Sally was startled by Tina. "Ooh," she yelled. And Sally quickly turned around and said, "Oh Tina, you frightened me," and she held her hand over her heart. Tina giggled as she said, "Where was your mind, girl? Huh?" Sally smiled and said, "Lost in files, I'm afraid." Tina held out her hands for a hug, and Sally quickly melted into them, and as Sally's breasts pressed against Tina's, a rush of excitement filled Tina's mind and she said, "Well, you sure looked cute bent over there." Sally blushed, and she ran her hand down Tina's back. Then she pulled away, and held Tina's shoulders, and she gave

Tina a sexy stare and she said, "I wanted to be certain that you started your morning out on the right foot." Then she gazed into Tina's eyes, and they both laughed.

While Tina didn't understand these new feeling, or her sudden attraction to women, she was thankful that Sally had exposed her to this exciting world. She was also thankful that she now had the ability to fantasize, but she knew, however, that she could never act on those fantasies, or at least she knew that she didn't want to. She was also thankful that she had talked with Sally, and set the rules. That makes it much easier, she thought, and helps us to know where the boundaries are, and it gives us freedom, without worry, of creating an unwanted situation.

Tina smiled, from excitement, thinking of their shopping trip during lunch as she said, "Oh Sally, I'm thrilled about our lunch date today. Where are you taking me?" As if she wanted to play a game, Sally said, "Now Tina, that's a secret." Then, like a school girl, Tina said, "Oh come on Sally. Give me a little hint. Please." Sally was having fun, torturing Tina, and she reached for her clip board as she said, "No, you'll just have to wait. I'm Sorry," and she giggled. Tina sighed, and remarked, in a disgusting tone, "Okay, it's only a few more hours. I guess I can wait that long." They wrapped their arms around each other's waists, as they giggled, and entered Tina's office.

Tina was seated at her desk, and Sally sat on the edge of it, and she glanced at her clipboard. Sally's short skirt, slid up high, on her thighs, and she slowly crossed her legs, and they looked inviting, and Tina's juices began to flow as she wondered if Sally knew what she was doing to her.

While Tina stared at Sally's legs, she thought. Nope, not for me. . . .Then her thoughts were interrupted as Sally spoke, "Let's see Tina. It looks like a light day. Mr. Ballard will be out all day, and you only have two messages, one from--" and suddenly, the phone rang. They stared at each other, and they smiled, and shrugged their shoulders, and Sally answered. "Burgers Inc., may I help you. Certainly Ms. Cunningham, hold one moment please." Sally held the phone to her breasts, and Tina fixed her eyes on them but abruptly Sally said. "Are you in?" Tina smiled as she reluctantly reached for the phone.

"Hello Ms. Cunningham, how are you today? Good, I'm glad to hear that, what can I do for you this morning?" Sally blew Tina a kiss, as she eased out the door, and Tina's eyes were glued to Sally's hot body, and she didn't want to miss a single move that Sally made, then Tina focused on her phone call as she said, "I'm sorry Ms. Cunningham, I was distracted, what was that again? No, I'm sorry; I haven't talked with our advertising department this morning. I'm not sure about the exact date of our promotion, but as far as I know, we're still on schedule....Don't be so nervous Ms. Cunningham, everything is fine. But please, make sure there are no delays on your end.... Oh no. I'm glad you called, communication is critical, call me anytime, please! Bye-bye Ms. Cunningham, have a wonderful day."

When Tina hung up, she took a deep breath, and she couldn't believe the excitement, Sally had aroused in her, simply by her mere presents. Tina was confused, but excited and hot, and she loved the feeling, but deep down, she was scared to death, and she didn't know what to do.

Her attention turned toward the business of the day, and she began checking her messages. Let's see, Ms. Cunningham, and she wadded that one up. Mr. Barnes. Okay. "Sally, get me Mr. Barnes please." "Right away Tina." Tina busied herself, tying up loose ends, before her trip Monday. "Tina, Mr. Barnes on line one." "Thanks Sally." Tina took a deep breath.

"Good morning Mr. Barnes, how are you today? Good, glad to hear it. . . . Oh great Mr. Barnes. I'm thrilled to hear you're ahead of schedule. . . . You're going to shoot tomorrow? Wow, that's great. No Mr. Barnes, I'm sorry, I'll be in Boston on Monday. I won't be back in the office till next Thursday. What time would you like for me to review the commercial on Thursday? Ten o'clock, that'll be fine. Great, I'll see you then. Oh, Mr. Barnes, by the way. Thanks for pushing this through for me. I'll see you Thursday. Bye now."

Wow, Thursday, she thought. "Sally." "Yes Tina?" Mr. Barnes will be here Thursday morning at ten o'clock. Will you make a note of that please?" "I certainly will, and by the way, are you ready for lunch?" Tina glanced at the clock, "Oh my gosh Sally, time got away from me. I didn't realize it was so late. Give me ten minutes, and I'll be right with you, okay?" "No problem Tina, I'll be waiting."

Tina's face lit up with excitement, and she hurriedly put her work away, and she quickly made her way to the door. As Tina left her office, Sally was setting on her desk, smiling, and clutching her purse. Tina smiled from ear to ear, and she moved next to Sally and she placed her hand on Sally's knee, and it felt warm, and tender, and Tina couldn't understand this sudden infatuation.

Tina wanted to take it into her hands, and hold it, and caress it, but she only patted it, and said. "Are you ready?" Sally slowly slid off her desk and she said, "I've been waiting." They giggled, and hooked arms, and they left the office.

After they negotiated the elevator, and made their way to the parking garage, Tina asked, "Okay Sally, where are we off to?" Sally winked at Tina, "No need getting into the car darling, we're going to Carmella's Boutique, just around the corner." A smile of excitement ran across Tina's face, as she thought, she had never been there before, but that she had always wanted to. Tina walked around the car, and like school girls they locked arms again, and began singing, were off to see the wizard, and they laughed, and walked the streets of Dallas, in search of Carmella's.

When they entered Carmella's, it was breath taking. The little shop was larger than Tina had expected, and the clothing, which was draped across the mannequins, was classy, and very seductive. Tina felt as though she had arrived at Disneyland, and she danced through the store smiling and humming a cheerful tune. Tina realized that for the first time in her life, she could buy seductive and revealing clothing, and the mere thought of that excited her. Then Sally called, "Tina, wait for me, I'm supposed to be helping, remember?" Sally laughed, as she chased Tina through the shop, and Tina held up a blouse next to her body, and turned around several times as she said, "Oh Sally, don't you just love it?" Sally moved next to her, and she took the blouse from her, and in a playful tone, she said, "Tina, this one is not right for you. What you're looking for is over here."

They weaved their way through the shop, until Sally finally came to a stop, and she said. "Here is what you're looking for." Sally held up a silk chiffon, wrap around blouse, and then she nodded to the mannequin next to them, which had the same blouse draped around it and Sally sheepishly said, "Sexy, huh?" "Gorgeous!" replied Tina. Just then, a saleslady appeared. "Good afternoon, may I be of assistance?"

She was a snooty, upper class, looking little lady, who was dressed to kill. Her smile didn't seem genuine, and she seemed more bothered by their presents, than glad to see them.

Sally broke the silence, as she rested her arm around Tina's neck. "Yes, this beautiful young lady needs an entire, new wardrobe."

"I see," the clerk said as her eyes gave Tina the once over. Tina and Sally stared into each other's eyes, and giggled. The clerk said, "My name is Irma, and I'll be glad to assist you." As the lady walked around the mannequin, Tina held her head high, closed her eyes, fixed a frown on her face, and she swayed her body from side to side, as if to mock the lady's snootiness. Sally roared with laughter, then she tried to refrain herself, but she couldn't, and Tina stopped mimicking the lady, and she tried to quiet Sally.

Finally, the two gathered themselves, and realized where they were. The lady gave them an odd stare and asked, "Are you interested in this blouse?" "Oh yes," replied Tina. "May I try it on?" "Of course, follow me please." When they reached the dressing room, Tina was handed the blouse, and she disappeared behind the curtain. The room was spacious, with an expensive sofa and elegant winged sitting chair. In Tina's excitement, she was so eager to try on the new blouse that she almost ripped hers off.

Tina wiggled around; trying to fit the blouse properly, then she glanced into the full length mirror, and she winked with approval, and rejoined Sally. When she entered the room, a radiant expression overtook Sally's face as she said, "Oh Tina, its breath taking. You're breath taking." Tina blushed as she asked, "Do you really think so?" The snooty lady smiled, and nodded yes. Sally rushed to Tina's side. "Turn around, my beauty, let me see it all." While Tina slowly turned around, she kept her eyes fixed on Sally, and she enjoyed Sally's excitement then Sally said, "OH honey, you are one fine lady." And Tina blushed again as she responded, "Thanks, and it feels so elegant." Sally giggled and had her hand covering her mouth as she said, "Believe me darling, on you, it's more than elegant. There's one small thing though." Sally took Tina's hand, and she led her into the dressing room.

When they passed through the curtain, Tina had a surprised expression on her face. "Honey," Sally remarked, "The only problem is, this blouse is designed to wear without a bra." Tina appeared stunned, and her mouth fell open, as she tried to speak, "Well, how will I--?" Sally began helping Tina pull the blouse from her skirt, and she giggled and said, "Don't worry, they won't fall out?" Then Sally moved behind Tina to help her slip the blouse off, and then she held it, and stepped back and watched, while Tina unfastened her bra, and flung it to the chair. The excitement of Sally's eyes scanning Tina's bare breasts, made her want to explode, and Tina turned to face Sally, and she wanted Sally to want them. Then Sally spoke, "Tina darling. I've got to hand it to you. You have really firmed up." Her eyes were wide open, and Tina realized that Sally's breath was taken away, by her beauty. Tina was proud to hear those words from Sally. After all the hard work, and sweat, and sacrifice, she finally realized, at that very moment, that she had made it. She finally had that new and sizzling hot body, that she had always dreamed of, and the wonderful woman, who made it possible, was standing before her, drooling over it, and that thought made Tina sizzle all the more.

Then she reached for the blouse, and Sally held it out, and Tina turned around, and seductively slid into it. While Sally fastened the blouse from the front, she slightly brushed against Tina's exposed breast, and Tina was sure it wasn't an accident, and she smiled, a devilish little smile, and she hoped Sally would brush against them again. "I'm sorry," Sally remarked, and she softly gazed into Tina's eyes, and then she continued to help.

Tina simply gazed back into Sally's eyes, and she watched Sally's every move, remembering the feeling she had last night, imagining Sally chewing on these very nipples, and she wished Sally would take one of them now, and caress it until she screamed. Suddenly, her nipples hardened, and Tina blushed, knowing they could be seen through the sheer material of the blouse, but she didn't give a shit, and she hoped that Sally would notice, and hoped that she would take it, but she didn't.

Sally slowly unzipped Tina's skirt, to tuck the blouse in, and Tina closed her eyes, to absorb every movement of Sally's fingertips. They felt like magic, as they moved down her body. Tina only pretended to help with the tucking, but actually, she let Sally do most of the work, so she could feel her hands against her hot body. The gentleness of Sally's hands moving against her skin, as she tucked the blouse in, brought Tina's excitement level to a peak, and when Sally moved behind Tina to tuck it in, her hands felt like magic. Tina could almost imagine how it would feel for Sally to squeeze her new little butt, and she wished she would, but she didn't, and Tina took a deep breath.

Tina's legs became wobbly, and her breathing became irregular, when Sally slid her hand against Tina's firm butt one last time. Sally noticed Tina's weakness, and she whispered over Tina's shoulder, "Are you okay?" Tina closed her eyes, and she smiled, and wished Sally would kiss her neck, just behind her ear and she said, "Hell yes! I'm in heaven." Then Sally moved close to Tina's side and she slowly began to raise the zipper on her skirt, and Tina gently closed her eyes one last time, to feel every movement of Sally's hands against her side.

Sally moved in front of Tina, and she caught Tina taking a glance down at her own breasts and Sally smiled as she said, "Honey, it's okay," and Sally giggled at Tina's apparent innocents, then she continued, "They're supposed to show, but I promise, they won't fall out."

Tina wished they would, then Sally took two steps back, to get a full view of Tina, and Tina began to model it, and she slowly turned around, and she knew she was arousing Sally, and she loved it.

Sally said, "Baby, it was made just for you. You look divine, and that's no bull shit!" Tina blushed, but she held her head high with renewed confidence as she said, "It feels wonderful," and with an embarrassed expression, she continued, "And when it rubs across my nipples. . . .Um. . . .It feels so sexy." Tina couldn't believe she said that, but she couldn't believe this new world she had been exposed to either and while this gorgeous blonde lady stood in front of her, Tina held her hand over her mouth and Sally laughed. "That's the whole idea honey. If you feel sexy, you'll be sexy, and believe me, you look delicious."

She knew Sally meant those words, and they made her feel beautiful, and if it weren't for the rules they had laid down, she would have taken Sally into her arms at that very moment, and experienced her hot luscious lips first hand.

Sally took Tina's hand as she said, "Come on, let's do some shopping." They giggled like schoolgirls until they faced Ms. Snooty Irma once again, then their demeanor changed to one of high society, and they strutted pasted her, toward another counter.

Then the clerk remarked, "Miss that blouse looks divine on you." Tina and Sally made eye contact, and they giggled, and Ms. Snooty continued. "What else may I show you this afternoon?" Sally immediately blurted out, "An evening gown, a dinner dress, and a short and sassy casual dress?" The lady had a surprised expression on her face, but she kept a stiff upper lip as she said, "And which would you like to see first?" Tina stood tall and said, "Let's begin with an elegant evening gown." Irma held her head high as she said, "Okay, this way please."

Tina held herself differently, with her seductive new blouse on, and Sally noticed immediately, and she leaned over toward Tina, and she whispered, "You look luscious." Tina nodded, while she followed Ms. Snooty to a rack of evening gowns, and she felt sexy, and she wiggled her butt for Sally's pleasure. Sally leaned over to Tina again and she softly said, "You'd better be careful!" Tina just smiled, and she felt hot, and she wanted to show off.

"These three racks are all your size," Ms. Snooty remarked. Sally darted in front of Tina, and she began brushing through the dresses, as though she knew exactly what she was looking for. Tina smiled and stepped back and watched, while Sally shuffled through them, and Tina became excited as she watched. Then Sally said, "Here it is," and she took it off the rack very carefully, as though she were afraid she may bruise it, and she held it up to Tina's already hot body and said, "Oh darling, I can't wait to see you in this. Hurry! Put it on." Tina could see Sally's excitement, when she handed Tina the dress, and encouraged Tina to hurry and put it on. Tina, enjoyed Sally's excitement, and she laughed at her as she said, "I'm going, I'm going!"

While Tina made her way to the dressing room, Sally was behind her all the way, and then Tina turned, and asked, with curious eyes. "No bra?" Sally closed her eyes and nodded, no. Tina disappeared through the curtains, wishing Sally would follow, but she didn't, and once again, she couldn't get out of her clothes quick enough. Her level of excitement was at an all-time high, as she flung her clothes on the chair.

Suddenly, she slipped her panties off, and flung them to the chair, and she became exhilarated, by the thought of standing in front of Sally, without them on. As she slid into the silky and seductive evening gown, her entire personality changed. Tina felt as though she were on fire. The dress was strapless, and cut just above her breast. She was amazed at the feelings she experienced, as the tight fitting dress hugged each curve of her body. Tina stopped in front of the mirror once again, and while she viewed herself, she noticed her mouth was wide open. For the first time, it finally struck her, of the awesome beauty she had captured for herself.

It's incredible, she thought, and she stood there in a trance. Then she smiled at herself, and gave herself a wink of confidence, and made her way through the curtain for a grand entrance.
Sally fell back against a counter with expensive clothing, and she tried to catch her breath. She placed her hand flat on her chest and tried to talk. "Tina....Darling.....You're so...." Then Sally looked at Ms. Snooty, to find her face was also lit up with excitement. Sally turned toward Tina once again and said, "Honey, you are lovely." Sally made her way to Tina, and she took her hand, and made gestures of catching her breath and she continued, "Baby, I mean it...I'm simply taken away with you. You are absolutely gorgeous."

Tina felt sexy, and full of life, and Sally's words and actions were an absolute turn on to her. Tina began to walk slowly back and forth, up and down the aisle, as if she was modeling her gown, but she was actually showing off her new sleek body, and Sally knew it. The twinkle in Tina's eyes highlighted the entire event, while Tina strutted her wears for Sally and Ms. Snooty. When she reached Sally, once again, Sally remarked, "Honey, you're incredible." Then Sally dropped to her knees and said, "But let me look at this, it may be too long."

Tina had an expression of astonishment in her eyes, as she stared down at Sally, in front of her, and on her knees. Tina wanted to reach down, and run her fingers through Sally's hair, but she just smiled, and let her imagination run wild. The dress was split down the middle, from the top to the bottom, with only a thin belt, keeping it fastened, and Sally folded the material underneath, at the bottom, as if to shorten the length, then she glanced at Ms. Snooty for approval. Ms. Snooty, made a face, and shook her head no, but Sally continued to work with it. "Something is not quite right," Sally said, "Let me see."

Tina only stared, while Sally ran her hand underneath the material, from her waist, to the floor. Sally pulled the dress apart at the split, searching for the problem. Holding one side of the dress outwards, to look inside, Sally's hand brushed against Tina's bare leg, several times, and the excitement began to build for Tina once again. She could imagine Sally's tongue against her inner thighs, searching for the sweet nectar between her legs, then she realized she had no panties on, and she hoped Sally wouldn't hold the dress any higher, and make the discovery. Then she smiled, and hoped she would. Her juices began to flow, while Sally prowled around underneath her dress, not even being concerned about rubbing against Tina's soft bare legs.

Finally, Sally placed her hand on Tina's inner thigh, inside her dress, and she ran it down to her ankle. Tina flinched with excitement, and Sally explained, "Ah Ha, I've found the problem." Tina closed her eyes, and held her head back, and she knew her peak was near. "It's your heels. The wrong sized heels." Tina thought, who gives a shit, just take me, silly. Now! Sally caressed Tina's ankle, when she made her discovery, and Tina squeezed her pelvic muscles together, and Sally laughed. "It's only your heels." Tina felt very uncomfortable, as she returned to reality, and she realized that she may have climaxed at that very moment. Tina shook her head, and squeezed her eyes, as if to say no, I can't do this. Not now!

She opened her eyes, and could feel the moisture between her legs, and then she smiled, and was amazed by the experience. She reached down with both hands, and she helped Sally to her feet, and she wanted to take Sally right then and there, but as their eyes met, they both smiled, and Sally said, "With the proper heels, this dress will be absolutely perfect on you, darling."

Tina realized that Sally was aroused and excited, and that thought excited Tina even more, and the word, darling, as Sally spoke it, at that very moment was the most beautiful word Tina had ever heard. Sally turned toward Ms. Snooty, to find her smiling, and nodding yes, in agreement. Tina smiled, and said, "I think you're right Sally." Sally giggled and said, "I know I'm right, baby, you look so lovely." Then she stepped back to get another glance, and the excitement on Sally's face said it all, she had the expression of a child on Christmas day, and Tina felt hot and weak in the knees as she spoke, "I don't mean to break up this party, but it's getting late. I need to change, if we're going to have time to look at anything else. Sally excitedly agreed, and Tina disappeared into the dressing room, where she collapsed on the sofa.

Tina's face was flush and her breathing heavy, but after a few seconds of gathering herself, she propped her legs up, and she couldn't resist any longer. Tina moved her hand against her leg, and she slowly ran it down to the juices between them. She found more sweet nectar than ever before, and it made her hot, simply to run her fingers through it.

Her thoughts were, Oh my God. This is so incredible. Then she dipped her fingers inside, and she brought them to her lips for a taste, and the sweetness of it surprised her. She returned her fingers, and inserted them, and with pleasure written all over her face, she squeezed her legs together, to enjoy the feeling for a moment.

It was the most incredible feeling, and the experience of her lifetime. I never thought a woman could make me feel the way I do, she thought, and then she smiled. Suddenly, she realized where she was. Oh my God, Sally and Ms. Snooty are waiting, and she quickly stood, and began changing clothes.

Before she returned to the outside world, she took one last deep breath, and then she walked through the curtains. Sally was smiling, when Tina appeared, and her expression was one of lust. Tina knew, at that very moment, that Sally really did love how she looked in the gown, and Tina walked with pride, next to her side, and they joined hands, and continued their search for Tina's wardrobe.

Once they returned to the office, Tina walked ahead of Sally, and she made her way, to the door of her office. In a seductive little tone, Sally said, "Tina, I love you, for what you gave me today." Tina turned and winked, and she pushed the door open, and she disappeared behind it.

Tina's smile could not be suppressed, while she had thoughts of the wonderful afternoon they'd had together, she began to realize she was falling in love with a woman. But not just any woman. This woman was the luscious and vivacious Sally.

CHAPTER 7

Warming up for Boston

Tina's level of excitement was almost unbearable, when she left Victoria's Secret, after work. It was difficult for her to divert her attention from Sally, as she made the short drive home, because each piece of lacy clothing that she walked out of Victoria's with, she selected with Sally in mind. For the first time, she could actually imagine the two of them together, and it was exciting. She could almost taste Sally's hot juicy lips, and she wished she could, and after today, she wasn't afraid anymore.

God! It's time to think about my date with Bob tonight, she thought. She dawned a serious expression, as she wondered how she would feel around a man, after the sizzling afternoon she had spent with Sally. Tina wondered if a man could ever replace what she experienced today. While her and Sally had never made love, just the simple thought of it, gave Tina an explosive feeling, one she had never experienced before, and one she was beginning to love and cherish. Tina was certain, however, that given the proper circumstances, it was possible, now, and it actually could happen. Tina wasn't afraid any longer, and she almost welcomed it, and craved it. Tina remembered Sally telling her, that after her first time with another woman, she couldn't get her off her mind, and now Tina understood exactly what Sally meant, and how she felt.

As much as Tina adored Bob, she almost wished she were spending the evening with Sally instead. Then she could experience the feeling of making love to a woman first hand, and there could never be another woman, better suited for Tina, than Sally.

Thoughts of Bob re-entered Tina's mind, and she realized, she had so much to do, and so little time to get it all done. As her house drew closer, she wondered what Bob would think about her new clothing, and the new Tina, underneath. He'll be very surprised, she thought, with a devilish smile on her face.

The next hour was filled with taking a shower, and primping, but as she slid her sleek new body, into the silky, seductive new dress she had bought, just for Bob, a rush of excitement filled her mind. While she gazed into the mirror, smiles danced across her face. Tina's new dress was fiery red, with a revealing, and plunging neck line. Her breast looked magnificent, as her dress caressed them, and hugged the curves of her sleek body, which ended just above her knees. She watched herself, in the mirror, lift her dress, and slowly wiggle out of her panties, and she almost exploded with excitement, by the thought of sitting next to Bob, at the restaurant, without a stitch underneath.

While she stood in front of the mirror smiling, and admiring herself, the doorbell rang. Oh my goodness, she thought, it's Bob. She wasn't ready for him to see her yet, so she went to the corner of the hallway, and called for him to come in. When he did, she ducked around the corner, and she called his name. "Hello Bob. Is that you?" Then Bob's voice could be heard as he said, "Yes baby, it's only me." Then Tina responded, "Bob, whatever do you mean by that?" Bob giggled and said, "Just kidding dear." Tina smiled at his humor, and she replied, "Just make yourself at home; I'll be out in a minute."

Tina returned to the mirror, and she was thinking how sexy and hot she felt, and the feeling of no panties was absolutely incredible. She strutted around, and watched herself in the mirror, and she convinced herself that Bob would be speechless. She made some last minute, final adjustments, before she made her entrance, then she peaked around the corner, into the kitchen, where Bob was hunched over the counter, thumbing through a magazine, while he waited.

She felt a little devilish, and she very quietly, tried to sneak up on him, in the same manner that she constantly tried with her daddy. The results were the same. In a loud voice, as if to call to her bedroom Bob asked, "Tina? Do you have mice? I can hear them in the kitchen." Tina giggled, and she stood straight up, and reached for his ribs, to tickle him. Bob began to laugh and jump as he said, "Tina. Don't! You know how ticklish I am." With his back still turned towards her, she wrapped her arms around him and said, "Oh Bob, you're no fun at all." He smiled, and replied, "Well, I certainly am! Your mother told me I was a lot of fun, so there."

While she held him, she realized his butt was a perfect fit for her crotch, and she wiggled it closer to him. Bob began to sniff the air in the room and he asked, "Honey, you have a new perfume, don't you?" Tina smiled, feeling proud that he had noticed and she answered, "I bought it just for tonight. Just for you my dear." Then he raised his arm, and he began to turn, so he could hold her in his arms, but as he did, he caught a glimpse of her fiery red dress and said, "Aha, a new dress too, I see?" Once he was completely turned around, and had a full view of Tina, her devilish little smile was tempting, and her breasts were gorgeous, and he couldn't take his eyes off them as he said, "Baby!"

He took her hands in his, and she stood back, with their arms stretched as far as she could stretch them, so he could have a good look. She released her hands, and took another step backwards, and she slowly spun around, for him to enjoy the entire package. She had her wish, because he couldn't speak, and the expression on his face was a mixed package. One of surprise, one of lust, and one of passion. When she stopped, she held out her arms to him and asked, "Well?" He gently closed his eyes, and then he reopened them and humbly said, "I'm in love. Baby, you look like a completely different woman." Then he eased into her arms, for a hug and he said, "You are so. . . and you feel so. . ."

Then he held her hands again, and he stepped back again, for another glimpse of her. Finally, a smile of approval ran across his face. "Baby, you're beautiful, you really are." She giggled, and blushed, then she pulled him closer, and their lips met, for the first time in over fifteen long years. Tina felt a rush of excitement, as his hands caressed her bare shoulders, then they moved down her back, and to her hips, and she knew he wanted to explore, and she let him. His lips were warm, and she ran her tongue across them, and the passion they both felt was too much for the moment, and she brought her hands to his chest, and she gently pushed him back, as if to say, that's enough for now.

Once their lips parted, his face was flush, and his eyes were closed, then he slowly opened them, and they had a twinkle of pleasure in them. Tina knew he had a thirst for her, and she for him, and she could feel the wetness between her legs, then she realized her panties were in her bedroom, and she became even more excited. He ran his hands slowly down the sides of her luscious body, from her breast, to her hips, then back up again. She closed her eyes in pleasure, to feel each movement of his fingers, and they dug into her skin, and he stared into her face, as his hands moved, and he knew he was pleasing her.

She slowly opened her eyes, and she pulled him to her bosom, for one last kiss. Then she whispered into his ear. "Darling, we've got to go." He kissed her on the cheek, and sighed a deep sigh as he said, "I know." And while he stared into her dark piercing eyes, which were searching his face for signs of any spot not excited, he said, "I don't remember us being this passionate." She giggled, and moved toward the counter as she said, "It's been a long time honey. I guess we've both grown up." He moved next to her side once again, and he took her into his arms, and he ran his hand down to her new little butt, then he patted it and said, "Too long." Then he smiled a devilish little smile.

Not wanting to start again, afraid if they did they wouldn't be able to stop, she motioned for them to leave. "Come on honey, there's plenty of time." She loved the way he was staring at her every move, and it made her feel hot, and seductive, and sexy. It made her feel like a woman, and like Bob, she hadn't remembered their past relationship being this heated.

Tina realized that Sally may have had something to do with that. Maybe her sudden infatuation with Sally didn't have anything to do with Sally. Maybe, Sally had simply awakened a sleeping giant within Tina, and aroused her sexually, by exposing her to new and exciting experiences. Maybe it was simply the sudden attention, and maybe it was simply the grueling workouts, that exhilarated her. Whatever the reason, she knew now, that those feeling were not simply confined to Sally. She was filled with the same, hot passion, while she was in Bob's arms, and she loved the feeling, and she craved his touch, and adored his starring eyes, and she wanted more.

Tina was confused, and she didn't understand her feelings, but she wanted to enjoy the moment, and she smiled, and felt as though the excitement of the night had just begun, and she was right.

Bob continued to glance at her during the entire trip to the restaurant, and they laughed, and told stories. She caught him taking subtle peeks at her legs, then her breasts, then her eyes, and she was hot with his interest in her. She became excited at the very thought of his searching eyes, and occasionally, she lifted her crossed leg, as if to reposition them, but she was actually, showing them off, and hoping he would take another peek. Then, the teasing became more intense. She slowly raised her hand, and gently rubbed the top part of her breast, in a nonchalant manner, while she looked away. She knew that Bob could take a good long look, knowing that she was not watching him, and he did, time after time, and it drove her wild with excitement.

She continued to play this hot little game with him. Occasionally she would slowly rub her knee, and then she ran her hand down to her bare ankle, and then she gently rubbed her upper breasts, and ran her hand up her neck, while she raised her head, and sighed. Tina knew that Bob's level of excitement was high, and she also knew that he was hot. She sneaked several peeks at his lap, and the swelling between his legs excited her all the more. They played this game of sneak-a-peek, all the way to the restaurant, like two teenagers on their first date. She knew he was aroused, and he knew she was, and when their eyes met, which was often, they smiled devilish little smiles, and then they turned away.

This exciting little game was soon over, when Bob turned into the parking lot of Oliver's restaurant and he stopped the car. Once he pulled the keys out of the ignition, he leaned over for another taste of her soft and fiery lips, and he rested his left hand around her waist, and he eased his right hand, behind her head, to gently pull her closer to him. She seductively, uncrossed her legs, and swung both her arms around his neck, and they kissed wildly, and passionately, and she wanted him to want more, and she pulled away, and kissed his nose and said, "Come on, you hot hunk, let's eat." Then she tickled him under his chin, with her finger, and she turned away, and opened her door.

He quickly opened his, and rushed to her side, and then he took her hand, and gently helped her out. She took one last opportunity to excite him, and as she slid out, her skirt rode up her thighs. When that happened, her entire legs were revealed, and he stared, and hungered for her, but being in the dark, he never noticed the very thing she wished he had. No panties. When she came to her feet, their eyes met, and he pulled her into his arms one more time. While they hugged, he whispered, "Baby, you are too exciting." She smiled, and they began their slow and deliberate walk inside.

Bob secured their table, and she decided to freshen up, and as she wiggled off, she knew he was watching, and she put an extra bounce in her step, and, an extra wiggle in her walk, and she disappeared into the crowd.

Before she left the ladies room, she took one last look at herself in the mirror, and then she smiled with pride because of her appearance. She was hot and juicy between her legs, and the feeling was exciting, but she didn't dare try to stop it, she only enjoyed it. Bob had been drooling, and she knew it. Tina knew that he loved the little show that she was putting on for him, and that excited her, and she decided to give him more. While she stood there, in front of the mirror, she brought her hands to her sides, and she ran them down to her hips, and she felt seductive, then she turned for the dining room.

Bob was anxiously awaiting her return, and she spotted him staring at her from a distance. She pretended to look away, and she let him enjoy her entire walk to the table, only glancing at him occasionally. Tina noticed the pleasure in his eyes, as she gracefully moved closer and closer to the table. Then she pretended to finally notice him, and she smiled with excitement, and stared into his eyes, then she briskly walked to his side. He stood, and took her hand into his, and he raised hers to his lips for a kiss, then he pulled her chair out for her, and she gracefully had a seat.

Bob scooted his chair closer to hers, and he had a seat, and he smiled at her. "I was afraid you had run away he said." Tina winked at him, and dawned a devilish little smile of her own and said, "Bob, I'd never run out on you, I love you too much." Bob smiled, and the waiter stopped by with a bottle of champagne on ice. Tina sensed that Bob was beside himself, and that he was captivated by her beauty, and she was excited by that thought. He gazed deeply into her eyes, and she was warmed by the gesture.

"Oh Bob, a bottle of the bubbly," and she placed her hand flat against her breasts, and pretended to be surprised. He watched her hand, as it snuggled between them, and she knew it, then his eyes were drawn to her smile and he said, "Why yes dear, after all, it's a bon voyage dinner. Remember? Boston?"

She became straight faced as she said, "Don't remind me, let me enjoy tonight." Her eyes gently closed, as if to savor each second of this night. He patted her hand, and he reached for the Champaign, and he began pouring a glass for each of them, and she watched his every move. Suddenly, the band began playing a soft melody, and his eyes were drawn to hers, and she winked at him once more, and it drove him wild.

They raised their glasses, and toasted each other, then she couldn't resist, and she sat her glass on the table and took his hand in hers and said, "Let's dance Bob." He couldn't be stopped, and he automatically stood, and raised her arm, and pulled her chair out for her to stand.

Everyone watched them, as they eased out to the dance floor, and they were the only couple dancing. They were so taken away with each other, they hadn't noticed the other people in the room, and then they held each other close, and they gazed into each other's eyes, as only lovers would.

She stood on her tiptoes, and kissed him behind his ear, and he pulled her close to his body, and they turned a full circle on the dance floor, and everyone applauded them.

Tina felt hot, and she pulled his body closer to hers, and as they moved to the music, his knee dug deeply into her panty-less crotch, and they both loved it, and she thought, if he only knew.

He gently kissed her bare shoulder, then her neck, and he drew her even closer, and everyone in the restaurant had their eyes glued to them, as they danced, oblivious to anyone else.

When the third song was about to end, their lips met briefly, and he leaned her low to the floor, with both arms gently wrapped around her, and their lips met for a passionate kiss, as the beautiful song struck its last note.

For a moment, there was a deafening silence. Then applause rang out, and the couple finally realized everyone had been watching. Tina blushed, and she took Bob's hand, and led him quickly to the table, and again, Bob pulled her chair out for her, and she was seated. At first, she wanted to crawl underneath it, but then she decided to enjoy the crowd's enthusiasm. Tina smiled and nodded, while cheerful and romantic remarks were tossed around the room.

Soon, the crowd calmed down, and everyone returned to eating and Tina said, "Bob? I never realized that you could dance like that." "Baby, you make it easy," and he smiled with pride, then he poured them another glass of champagne. "Well, I absolutely love it." Then she leaned closer to Bob, almost in a confidential way and she whispered, "It really turns me on." Bob gained a serious expression, and he took her hand, and he giggled as he said, "Well then, come on baby, let's dance some more." She laughed out loud and said, "Not this very second silly, I want to enjoy this wonderful champagne, and gaze into your eyes. I've never felt closer."

They had been at the restaurant for forty-five minutes, before the waiter could catch them, idle enough, for them to order, and they laughed about it, while they helped each other with their selections. Once they finished ordering, the waiter remarked, "We don't often find a married couple, so much in love, as you two are, and you were great fun to watch, on the dance floor."

She reached for Bob's arm, as the waiter walked away, and she gazed into his eyes, and they laughed at his remarks, then she pulled him closer, and she kissed his cheek. "Thanks Bob, you're wonderful." Bob stared into her eyes and he said, "You're the wonderful one at this table, and just watching you move, is a real turn on for me." Tina blushed, and she gazed at the burning candle on their table and she said, "Oh Bob." Then silence surrounded the table, and the only sounds to be heard, were those of forks clanking against plates, and the hustle and bustle of people moving from here to there. The busy restaurant continued around them, and thoughts of Bob and Tina's past filled her mind.

Tina remembered them briefly dating fifteen years ago, and how very unromantic the relationship had seemed at that time. Then, she transferred to another college. Tina remembered their vows to always remain close friends, no matter how many miles separated them. Then her thoughts turned to their relationship of today, and how well they were getting along, as her daddy put it. She silently thought how warm and comfortable she felt in his presents, and how much fun they always seemed to have, constantly joking and laughing about any and everything. Tina had always felt a very close bond between them, but tonight. . .Well, tonight was different. Tonight was new to their relationship, and very exciting, she thought. Very exciting.

Bob caressed Tina's hand, realizing she was lost in thought, and the burning candle held her in a trance, then she smiled, and turned to him, and the reflection of the candle was shining in her eyes and she asked.

"How do you suppose our relationship would have turned out, if we had stayed together all those years ago?" A puzzled expression ran across Bob's face, and he wondered where that question had come from, then he peered into her eyes, and slowly shook his head no, and shrugged his shoulders. "I have no idea baby."

Then he was swept away with the same thoughts as her, and softly, she asked, "Do you think we would have married?" and she wrinkled her nose. Bob giggled, but he didn't answer that question, instead, he searched his mind, for a moment before he said, "Honey, I'm just happy the way things are at this very moment. If our past had been different, our present wouldn't be what it is at this very second, and honestly, I've never felt closer either."

A tear of joy filled Tina's eyes, and she heard the words she had hoped to hear, and she lifted his hand, and softly kissed it and said, "I love you Bob." And he quickly replied, "And I love you Tina. I always have." Tina drew his hand to her neck, and she cuddled it, and she rested her cheek against it, and closed her eyes, to savor the moment, but the waiter interrupted with their meal.

She was startled by him, and she jumped, and she was suddenly brought back to reality, and broken away from her closeness to Bob, and his loving thoughts.

While the waiter quietly served the meal, Tina and Bob's eyes never lost contact, and they never noticed the movement of the waiter, while he placed piles of food before them. Her eyes were in constant motion, and they scanned Bob's face. Tina took in Bob's beautiful brown eyes, so big and bright, his gorgeous slim nose, those full luscious lips, and his strong chin, with the tiny scar he received while playing football in high school.

Bob's dimples were the highlight of his face, they're what made him so damned irresistible, and the way he carried himself was enough to cause most women to succumb, but it's his inner thoughts she loved the most. The way Bob expressed himself, and gazed deeply into her eyes is the one thing that Tina adored. Then she thought, his since of humor was certainly nothing to overlook, and she smiled at him, and thought, he's a hell of a man.

Soon, the waiter completed his task, and Tina and Bob's eyes were still fixed on one another, when the waiter broke the silence and asked, "Will there be anything else?" Bob looked up at him with starry eyes and said, "Huh?" Then he came to his sense's, realizing where he was. "Oh, I'm sorry. No that will be all, thank you." Tina smiled at Bob and sheepishly said, "I'm not!" Bob asked, "Not what, dear?" Tina said, "I'm not sorry."

Laughter returned to the table during the meal, and Tina and Bob put their passion for one another aside for a while. But they both felt that passion, and they knew those feelings could be summoned very easily, and very quickly, while they enjoyed the other sides of one another.

Tina and Bob had the look of lovebirds, as they finished their meal, and they hardly took their eyes off one another. It was very clear to them both, that love may be in their future, but not a word was spoken of it, while the endless gazing continued.

Before long, Bob reached for his credit card, and her eyes were glued to his every move, and as he glanced at her, she gave him a seductive wink and he smiled as he received it.

When they strolled from the table, they received stares from everyone in the restaurant, admiring their apparent, deep love for one another. Bob and Tina never noticed, and he rested his hand, flat on her back, to guide her out the door, and into the Fourier.

When he opened the door, they noticed a very light drizzle, which reflected off the wet asphalt, and it gave the surroundings a fairytale appearance, to cap off this already perfect moment.

He leaned down for a taste of her calling lips, and they scampered to the car, like school kids, where he opened her door, and she quickly slid inside.

She leaned over to open his door, and as he eased into his seat, he caught a sexy glimpse of her right leg, as she lifted it while reaching over the console and it was beautiful.

Tina giggled, when Bob started the car and she said, "Darling, you're all wet." He poked his finger against her ribs, and she let out a squeal and he playfully said, "Take that." Then she reached over, and tickled his ribs, and he laughed so hard, he could hardly catch his breath and he said, "Stop, please stop, I give up." But she was relentless with her payback, and she continued for a moment, but she finally stopped when she felt he'd had enough.

It took him several minutes to recover, and as he tried to catch his breath, and stop laughing, she reached over with a tissue, to dry his tears. "Poor baby," she uttered. "You shouldn't mess with the wild animals." He laid his head on the headrest, while he caught his breath, and he began to recover, then he turned to her with a smile and he shook his head yes as he responded, "With the emphasis on wild!" Tina poked his ribs with her finger, once again, as she said, "Alright buddy, watch it." And at that very moment, she realized she couldn't be happier.

Once they arrived at Tina's house and she unlocked the front door, she invited Bob in for a glass of wine, and he uttered. "A quick one, I'm leaving on my business trip to Houston early in the morning, remember?" Tina quietly said, "Oh yeah, I almost forgot." She opened the refrigerator, to take out the bottle of wine, and as she poured, she made the comment, "I wish you didn't have to go." Bob answered, "I know baby, but four a.m. comes awfully early." Tina said, "True, but I meant, I wanted you here with me, when I leave for Boston, Sunday."

He moved next to her side, and he wrapped his arm around her waist. Tina replaced the cork back into the bottle, and then she turned around, and took him into her arms, as if she never wanted to let him go. Bob said, "Honey. It's okay," and he patted her back, and she began to cry soft little tears of joy, as she remarked, "Something happened tonight. Something very special." Then she stared into his eyes, and he wiped the tears from them and he said, "It happened to me to… and feels good doesn't it?" and he shook his head yes, as if to convince her to do the same.

Tina giggled, and she stared into his eyes as she responded, "Good is not how I would describe it. It's more like incredible, warm, exciting, exhilarating, earth shattering--" They both became playful again and Bob blurted out, "Okay, okay, that's enough with the expletives. You don't want to overdo it." "I'm not over doing it," she said as she smiled. Then she continued, "That's how I honestly feel, and you didn't let me finish, it's also scary." "Scary?" Bob asked.

Then Tina pulled away from his arms, and she strolled to the sliding glass doors, leading to her deck, where she opened the curtains, and leaned against the glass. "Yes, scary, she said. I've always cherished our relationship, and I never wanted to do anything to change it, but after tonight. . . well, I don't know."

He moved next to her, and leaned against the glass, and he starred deeply into her eyes as he said, "Please don't be afraid baby." "I've loved you from day one, and I've always dreamed you'd feel the same way, someday.

I've been waiting a long time," he said. Tears came to her eyes, and she reached to him, and ran her hand up and down his arm as she said, "I never knew that darling, you never--" Bob interrupted as he said, "I know, I never felt I had the right. Since our fling in college, I've cherished what we've had, and I was afraid to say anything, afraid I'd destroy it."

Tina took him into her arms, and as they hugged, they swayed back and forth and Tina said, "I love you Bob, but I need some time with this. Everything is happening so fast."
 She leaned back to gaze into his eyes, then she moved her lips, as if to say, "I love you." He ran both of his hands down her arms, then back up again as he said, "Take your time baby. It's already been fifteen years, and I'd wait another fifteen, if need be. But right now, I have got to go. I'm sorry I can't be with you Sunday, but I'll certainly be thinking of you."

Bob brought his hot lips to hers, and the passion erupted. Her hands slid down to his butt, and she found herself pulling him closer to her body, to feel his crotch against hers. In his excitement, she felt his erection, and it became larger, and larger in his pants, and she wanted it, and her juices began to flow, but she pulled away, thinking not now, not like this.

She shook her head no, and she stepped away from him as she said, "Bob, what I feel for you is stronger than lust. God only knows how much I want you." She peered into his eyes, and hers were filled with tears. "I love you Bob, but I need time to think. When the day comes, that we make passionate undying love, it'll be for the right reasons, and not because of lust."

Bob moved next to her, for a taste of her lips, which were wet with tears and he said, "Baby, that's why I love you. I must go now." They held hands, and strolled toward the door, and she remarked, "I don't suppose I'll be seeing you again, until Thursday, when I get back from Boston." Her expression was sad, as she continued. "That'll give us time to think." Then she devoured his lips, and he slid out the door toward his car. With tears in her eyes, she watched Bob disappear into the night.

CHAPTER 8

Home and Family Are My Blessings

While Tina stared at the luggage that she packed for her trip she thought, that's a lot of stuff for only three days, and then she shook her head no as she realized it was all necessary. She plopped on the edge of her bed, and she was glad to have that job out of the way, then once again, her mind was filled with thoughts of Bob. While she lay back on her bed, and stared at the ceiling, she could feel the warmth of his arms holding her tight. Tina remembered his laughter in the car Friday night, when she tickled his ribs. She smiled at the thought of his loving words, "I've waited fifteen years, and I'll wait fifteen more, if I need to. Let's see she thought, Tina Evans that sounds pretty darn good. Tina Evans, Tina Evans, Yep, it sounds damn good, as a matter of fact.

Then she tried to imagine how life might be, if they were actually married. Let's see, I'll make him breakfast each and every morning. Would I really?. . . Yes, I would! Each morning before work, we'd stop at the doorway, for a passionate kiss. Would we really?. . . Absolutely! Then we'd meet at a restaurant for lunch. Would we really?. . . Nah-- We'd meet at home for lunch! Then she rolled with laughter.

She couldn't help herself, as she imagined coming home next Thursday, and melting into his arms, then taking a step back, to search his eyes, and utter the words. "Bob, I love you, and I would love to be your wife." Then she visualized him sweeping her into his arms, and carrying her off to never-never-land, where they would live happily ever after.

Wow, she thought, can that really be? Could we really be that happy? Then, thoughts of her parent's relationship ran through her mind. She smiled thinking of how incredibly happy they were, and how full their lives were, and how wrapped up in one another they were, and how much in love they were. Could Bob and I be so lucky, she thought, then she stood, and began to pace as she thought. Could we enjoy half the happiness my parents have, or would we end up like so many others?

When she made her way to the kitchen for her second cup of coffee, the word children ran through her mind. What about children? I'm thirty-seven, and Bob is thirty-nine, are we too old? If we had a child next year, when it is ten, I'll be forty-eight and Bob would be fifty. I don't know about that. Do I really want to chase kids around the house? I'd have to give up my job. Could I? Would I?

Being a wife means many changes to my life, but being a mother means many more. I know that I think I want to be married but do I really? Being lonely is not a good enough reason for getting married. Getting married really means giving my life to someone else. Giving it away, totally, and completely, just like my mom has.

She smiled, and thought, that's how they've done it. While my daddy is great with her, she's the one who has pledged her life to the marriage. She has always been right there for him, in any and everything that he wanted, or needed. She has always made sure that he was content, and in that, she found contentment.

Tina moved into her den, and she sat in the recliner, and she brought her feet up, and snuggled into a little ball, and thought. Wow, can I do that? Can I be that strong? Then thoughts of Bob came to mind, again. What kind of husband would he be? He's a whole lot like my daddy. He's extremely thoughtful, he's kind, he's generous, and loving. That man doesn't have a selfish bone in his body.

Tina remembered the time, when she had missed work for a solid week because of the flu. Bob stopped by each morning, to make sure I was doing okay. Then he gave up his lunch each day, to come over, and heat up chicken soup for me. After work, he'd come by to check on me again, and to feed me, and to make sure I was comfortable, and he didn't miss a day. During one of those days, she remembered, she was so sick, and her temperature was so high, that he spent the night on the couch, just in case, she needed him.

He sends me cards for every occasion. My birthday, he hasn't missed that one. . . . Ever! She thought. And once, I had a water pipe burst underneath my house, one winter's day. I still don't know how he found out about it, but he came driving up in his old work truck, with his tools, and he crawled under my house to fix the problem. He was under there for more than an hour, she thought, and when he crawled out, he was soaking wet, and covered in mud. He was freezing, and I spread newspapers on the floor in front of the fireplace for him to warm himself, and I pumped hot chocolate down him, until finally, he was revived.

She remembered the time, shortly after college, when she was in between jobs, and she couldn't afford to pay her rent, or the utility bill, or the phone bill, or even eat. She lived in Sherman Texas, and he lived in Tustin California, but somehow word traveled to him that she was in need, and he sent her a cashier's check for a thousand dollars, and a note. Don't worry about a thing, you're a bright woman, and you'll get past this rough spot in the road. Love Bob.

Suddenly, she was shaken by the ringing of her phone, and those sweet thoughts of Bob faded, as she answered. "Why hello mom." Tina sat up straight, and she smiled from ear to ear. "I'm so glad you called. I know mom, my plane leaves at six o'clock, so I've got about seven hours, but fortunately, all my packing is finished, and I guess I can just, hang out, until then." And she giggled. Then with a surprised tone, she answered. "I'd love to have lunch with you and daddy. Yes mom, a late lunch would be perfect. Okay, I'll see you at three o'clock. I love you, bye-bye."

Her happy expression soon turned sad, when she thought of her trip to Boston, and those three long and boring days, and those lonely nights. The sooner I get there, the sooner I'll get back, she thought, then she slid out of the recliner, and she eased into the kitchen, to rinse her cup.

Tina Evans, she thought, (and then she said it out loud. "Tina Evans." You know, that sounds better and better every time I hear it. Then, once again, she was swept away with her thoughts of Bob.

As the afternoon flew by, she found herself drying off, after her shower, and she glanced at the clock, and it was two-fifteen. My parents will be here soon, she thought, then she caught a glimpse of her new body in the mirror, and she stood motionless for a moment. Her face was filled with disbelief, while she stared at each and every curve, then she moved into her bedroom and in front of the full length mirror, for a better look.

She felt sexy, and confident, almost like a different woman. Then her thoughts turned to Sally, and the feelings Tina felt for her the past couple of weeks. She sat nude on the edge of her bed, and she continued to stare in the mirror, and she remembered the night that she conjured up, with Sally. Through the many fantasies, she'd had the past several weeks, the ones of her and Sally together was the hottest, and the most exciting ones of all. She laid back into her bed, and propped one leg up, as she stared at the ceiling, thinking of Sally and her fantasies of them together. She folded her arms, across her breasts, and she began to slowly shake her head no, as she realized she'd never be able to feel Sally's, naked body, next to hers, and she'd never really know for sure, how warm and soft Sally's lips really are.

She suddenly sat up, and she decided it didn't matter, and it was probably better that way. The experiences she had conjured up in her mind, of her and Sally caressing each other weren't real, they were only fantasies, but boy did they seem real, and feel real, she thought. A determined expression crossed her face, and she nodded yes. I can live with that!

She glanced at her clock again, and it was two-forty, and she jumped up, from her bed, as if she was on fire.

I'd better hurry, mom and dad will be here any minute, and just as she was putting the finishing touches on her makeup, the doorbell rang, and she darted to the door, in her bare feet.

She stood tall, took a deep breath, smiled, and opened the door, to find no one there. She opened the security door, to get a closer look, and as she stuck her head out, she heard her daddy's voice, "Boo!" She jumped about ten feet, and placed her hand flat against her chest, as if to gather herself.

"Daddy, that's not fair. You never let me scare you like that." James laughed, and he reached out his arms for a hug. "Well Cupcake. I'm sorry, but you're simply too easy." She pulled away, and reached out to hug Joan, and James disappeared into the house. "Hi mom, I'll never know how you put up with that man!" Joan giggled as she said, "It's easy dear, I love everything about him."

The girls locked arms, and went into the house, only to find James carrying Tina's luggage past them. "I hope everything is in order," he said, "and I hope these bags are ready for me to load." "They are daddy, all but the little one on my bed."

While James loaded the luggage, the girls strolled to the kitchen, where Joan opened the refrigerator door, and she helped herself to a glass of orange juice. "How've you been dear?" Tina smiled. And she replied, "Just fine." And Tina snuggled close to Joan. "Mom, I know you love Bob to death, but. . . What do you think of?... Well. . . ." Joan smiled, and interrupted her. "You mean what do I think of you and him, as a couple?" Tina's face shown bright and she was glad that Joan had helped her out. "Yeah, how did you know?" "It's quiet obvious dear; you love him too, don't you?" Tina hung her head, and she walked away from Joan, and she could be heard saying, "I don't know." And Tina looked at Joan with a puzzled expression.

Joan moved next to Tina, and with a twinkle in her eyes she said, "You know, I love Bob. And your father, well, you know how he feels too, but you're doing the right thing, by thinking about it. I mean, I know you love Bob, but there are so many things to consider. That is, if you're asking me about marriage."

Tina nodded yes, and then Joan took Tina's chin in the palm of her hand as she quietly said. "But honey, don't be so sad. Instead, you should be thrilled. This decision of yours should be fun for you, not painful. But honey, you know I'm prejudice." Tina nodded yes. "I think Bob is the most charming young man I've ever met, and I don't think, you could ever make a better choice. But you must search your own heart and soul, to make absolutely certain, you're ready for that kind of a commitment."

A rush of happiness ran across Tina's face and she hugged Joan. "You know, just a few weeks ago I was desperate to get married, but now that my choice is clear, I'm hesitant, and I don't understand." Joan hugged her, and smiled. "There's no rush, you've waited this long." Tina smiled. "Thanks mom, I knew I could count on you."

Just then, James stood in front of them, patting his foot. "Alright ladies, what's going on here? I've loaded the luggage, and with every trip I've made, you two were hugging each other. Now, I'm hungry, so if this isn't important, can we please take it to the car?"

Tina gave James a hug. "Let me get my hand bag, big guy." "Big guy?" James snickered. "I've been called a lot of things in my days, but, big guy hasn't been one of them." He laughed, and he reached out his arm, for Joan, and she snuggled against his side, as they made their way to the front door. "Is she okay?" he whispered. "Better than you know," Joan replied.

James had decided on a little restaurant, just a few miles from DFW airport, and the trip there was spent in laughter. When James turned into the parking lot, Tina was trying to recover from a joke he had told them.

"Oh daddy, you're so silly." Then she glared at Joan and asked, "Mom, where does he get this stuff?" Joan giggled and said, "I don't know dear, I think he was born that way?" Tina giggled and blurted out, "That's so sad, just thinking of being doomed to a life of constant laughter, makes me... well... it makes me laugh." Both James and Joan began laughing at Tina, and James remarked. "Now look at who's being goofy." "Oh help me!" Tina blurted out, while she tried to dry her tears of joy, and gather herself. "Help me Lord, this man is crazy," she yelled.

The laughter could be heard across the parking lot, and Tina wedged herself between the two of them, and she wrapped her arms around their waists as they got out of the car, and they strolled to the steps of the restaurant.

The instant they entered, Tina spotted one single rose in a glass vase, sitting on the hostess counter, with a card hanging from it, and in red marker, was written, "Tina Hargrove". She quickly reached for the card, and looked at the hostess, and asked, "Is this for me? I'm Tina Hargrove." The hostess smiled, and nodded yes.

Tina took the card, and read it aloud. "Thinking of you, have a safe flight. Bob."

Tina became teary eyed, as she reached for the rose, to sniff its beauty, while Joan and the hostess simultaneously said, "Ah isn't that sweet?" Tina reached for James, for a hug, and as they hugged, he remarked, "Nice guy." She glared up at James, and replied in a scolding sort of way. "He's better than a nice guy daddy, he's wonderful." James kissed her cheek, and gazed into her eyes, as he replied, "It's good to hear you finally admit that Cupcake." Tina caressed her rose, stuck her tongue at James, and she took Joan's hand. "Come on mom, let's eat."

When the hostess seated them, Tina sat her rose in front of her, and her smile was only equaled, by the glow on her face. She shook her head, as if to say, no, "Mom, what am I going to do with Bob?" Joan smiled and said, "You'll figure it out dear, don't worry."

James snickered. "I can think of a few things! For one, you could marry him, before he gets away." Tina dawned an expression of disgust, and she playfully hit his arm. "Daddy, it's been a long time, and he's still here. I don't think he's going anywhere."

James was hoping she would say that, and he went, for the kill. "You see! That's my point exactly. He's been around for a long time. Doesn't that tell you something, he's a very good man, he's very loyal, very dependable, very honest and I for one like the man."

Tina only stared at her rose, as she thought about that statement, and she realized that James was right. Even Bob himself had said it. "I've waited fifteen years."

And it was true, he had. He was always there for her, and she hadn't really realized that, until now.

All of a sudden, the question wasn't, did Bob love Tina? It was very clear to everyone that he absolutely did. Instead, it was the other way around. Did she love him? She knew she did, but with her new feelings toward Sally, and the sudden, rekindling of her relationship with Bob, her emotions were jumbled, and she just didn't know what she felt.

James patted her hand and said, "I was only kidding, Cupcake. You can't marry a guy just because he sends you a flower." Tina was surprised to hear him say that, and she knew he didn't really feel that way, but right now, she was more interested in how she felt.

"Daddy? Why did you marry mom?" James shrugged his shoulders, and giggled. "Because I love her." Tina smiled as she said, "I know that, but how did you know she was the right woman for you?" Joan smiled, and she leaned forward, anxious to hear his answer, and James repositioned himself, and he sat straight up, and giggled as he said, "Gosh honey, you do love him don't you? She poked his ribs, and he jumped, and laughed and said, "Just answer the question!"

He became serious, and Joan and Tina, watched him thinking it over, as they anticipated his answer. Before long, a smile crossed his face, as the answer came to him, and he leaned toward Tina.

"Well, Cupcake. I could have married your mother because of her beauty," and Joan blushed as he continued, "Or I could have married her because of her wonderful personality." He paused for a moment and then said, "And I could have married her, because of all the things she does for me, or because of what she means to me. But I didn't."

Joan and Tina were on the edge of their seats, and James sensed their anticipation, and he had them right where he wanted them.

"I married your mother, because my heart told me, it was the right thing to do." He smiled, and Joan blushed, and Tina said, "Ah Daddy. You're just perfect. Do you know that?" He lowered his head, and giggled as he said, "Yeah." Tina quickly slapped his shoulder, and they laughed.

Tina smelled her rose again, and suddenly, a strange expression crept across her face as she said, "Hey! How did Bob know we were coming to this restaurant anyway?" She stared into James' eyes with an accusing expression. "Huh?"

James wanted to hide underneath the table, but he knew he couldn't, and he said, "Okay, I give up," and he raised his hands in the air, and giggled as he admitted, "Bob called this morning, and he set the whole thing up." Tina took a deep breath and said, "Sure, that's right; blame it on Bob, since he's not here to defend himself." They giggled, and Tina fondled her rose, and she had a twinkle in her eyes, as she thought of all the trouble and planning Bob had gone through, to see to it that her departure was perfect. James realized she was in another world, as he blurted out. "You don't look very upset to me." Then very softly, Tina replied, "Oh daddy, if you only knew."

Tina seemed preoccupied with her rose all during lunch, and as they strolled back to the car, she held the vase tightly against her breasts, and the rose stood out for her nose to smell it, at will. Joan and James left her alone, lost in her thoughts of Bob, while they made the short drive to the airport.

When they arrived at DFW airport, James summoned a porter, and Tina and Joan made their way inside. The crowd was enormous, and loud, and Tina knew they couldn't wander too far, in fear of losing James, but she needed a moment alone with Joan.

As the girls strolled away from the doors, Tina turned to Joan, and said. "It's a beautiful flower."

"Yes it is, but I'm surprised it has any peddles left on it, the way you've held it next to you, all this time," and they giggled. Joan realized that Tina was in the middle of making the most important decision of her life, and she pulled Tina into her side, and she hugged her, and as she stared into Tina's eyes, she softly said. "Give it a few days honey. Just give it a few days. When the time is right, you'll know." Tina smiled, and nodded yes.

"You know mom, I really admire you and daddy. If I thought for one minute that Bob and I could have what you have, I wouldn't hesitate." "I believe you can honey. He's a good man. But you'll have to sort that out for yourself." Tina shrugged her shoulders as she said, "I know," then she gazed deeply into Joan's eyes, "You've been a great help Mom, thanks"

They turned to face the doors, and they saw James searching for them. Tina smiled, and nudged Joan, and then she pointed toward James. "I wonder who that man's looking for?" Joan giggled and said, "I don't know. Do you think we should rescue him?" Tina giggled, "Yeah, let's go."

The three of them casually strolled to the security area, and laughter prevailed, as James seemed to be on top of his game, and funnier than ever. Thoughts of his upcoming birthday crossed Tina's mind, and she gazed into his cheerful eyes, and then her mom's. She visualized the happiness, he would experience, when he saw the wonderful gift that his wonderful wife had gotten him. They're two very special people she thought, and she was lost in the warm feeling it gave her.

When the announcer, at Tina's gate, called her flight number, she stood, and turned toward James for a hug, and he said, "Be careful in Boston Cupcake. I'll see you Thursday. And by the way, I'll keep an eye on Bob for you." And they laughed and Tina said, "I love you daddy, bye-bye."

Tina turned toward Joan, and she held her tight, and she whispered into her ear, "I love you mom, thanks for the talk." Joan squeezed Tina and said, "I love you too darling, and I'm always here for you." Tina giggled, as she thought of James, and she said, "Keep this guy under control. Will you?" They laughed as Joan said, "Don't worry, I will." Tina eased away from them, and Joan blurted out, "Tina! Be careful dear. We love you," and Joan and James held hands, like high school sweethearts. When Tina reached the boarding area, she turned, and waved bye, and blew them a kiss, then she disappeared into the crowd.

CHAPTER 9

The Charm of Boston

The flight to Boston was pleasant, and as the plane touched down, thoughts of Samuel Morrison flooded Tina's mind. He's supposed to have a limousine driver meet me here, and take me to the hotel, she thought, I hope I can find him. This Samuel Morrison character must be a rich and classy guy, if he can throw his money around on limousines, and drivers, and hotels. I can't wait to meet him, and she gathered her things, and slowly made her way through the crowd, to the arrival area.

She immediately noticed a well-dressed, middle-aged man, holding a sign with her name on it, and she fixed a smile on her face, and she moved closer to him." Hello, I'm Tina Hargrove," she remarked. "Hello Ms. Hargrove, my name is Eric, and I'll be driving you to the hotel." They made their way to the baggage claim area, where he loaded her luggage, and they were whisked away by the Boston traffic.

During the trip, Eric had his back glass down, so they could talk with each other, if Tina felt the need. "Excuse me Eric, which hotel will I be staying in?" "The Hilton, Ms. Hargrove." She often stayed at The Hilton, on many of her trips, and she was glad that Mr. Morrison had the same standards.

"Eric, tell me about Mr. Morrison," and she sat on the edge of her seat, anxious to hear what Eric had to say. "Well, Ms. Hargrove, he owns a multi-million-dollar company, which he founded fifteen years ago. His company is diversified, and it's made up of many smaller companies, such as yours." "Interesting," she remarked. "What kind of man is he?" Eric smiled. "He's a very nice man, and fun to do business with, but he's also stubborn." "Stubborn?" she questioned. "That's how he's made his money, Ms. Hargrove; he's very picky about which business he invests in." "I see." And she began to plan her tactics that she would use during their meeting.

"When will I meet, Mr. Morrison?" "Tonight, Ms. Hargrove. He'll call your room, after you're settled, and meet you in the lounge for a drink." "He doesn't waste any time does he?" And she slid back into her seat. "No ma'am, you'll find Mr. Morrison to be on top of most everything he's involved with."

She enjoyed the short trip through downtown Boston, but she became nervous about meeting Mr. Morrison. He's becoming more intriguing by the minute, she thought. Fifteen years ago. Hum. He founded his company while I was still in college, and she realized her earlier visions of Mr. Morrison, were totally in left field. He's not forty, as she had fantasized, and he's stubborn too.

Before long, Eric pulled the beautiful, black, limousine in front of the elegant Hilton, which would be her home for the next three days. When he opened the door for Tina, he handed her, the key to her room. Tina glowed, as she said, "Thank you Eric." He smiled and closed the door behind her, and he quickly walked around the limousine, and began unloading her luggage.

"Good evening Ms. Hargrove." The doorman remarked. "I trust you had an enjoyable trip." "Very much so," she replied. And as they approached the elevator, the doorman remarked "Nice to have you with us, Ms. Hargrove, we'll send your luggage to your room right away." Tina nodded, and smiled. "Thank you."

Her room was gorgeous as expected, but her breath was taken away, when she noticed several bouquets of freshly cut flower arrangements, on the table, across from her bed. She excitedly tipped the bellboy, and thanked him, and she saw him out, then she quickly returned to the flowers, to read the cards.

"Hope the room is adequate. Samuel Morrison." Tina turned around, and she leaned against the table, as she thought, that's sweet. Then, she turned around again, and opened the next card. "Hope your trip was enjoyable. I'm anxious to meet with you. Jonathan Morrison. "Hum, she thought. I wonder who Jonathan Morrison is. She shrugged her shoulders, and turned her attention to the lavish flower arrangements, thinking how gracious, and thoughtful, and generous the two men had been. Guess I'll find out soon enough who Jonathan Morrison is, she thought, as she enjoyed the tantalizing smell which filled the room.

She stepped back, and began slowly undressing, and she gazed at the sight, and as she pulled her blouse, from her skirt, she noticed another small vase hidden behind the others. She quickly moved to the side of the table, and reached for it, and she brought the single red rose to her nose for a smell. She set it on the table, and excitedly fumbled with opening the card. It read.

"I can't wait to see your beautiful face on Thursday. Thinking of you. Bob." She brought her hand to her chest, and gasped for air, as she was taken away, with his kindness. She picked up his rose, and danced with it across the room, where she finally collapsed on the edge of her bed. Tears filled her eyes, and a smile of joy crossed her face, and her mind was filled with wonderful thoughts of Bob.

She set the vase on the night stand, and took the rose from it, and she lay back on the bed, and caressed it. "Oh Bob, what am I going to do with you?" Then she brought the rose to her nose once more, and she smiled from ear to ear, as she took in the aroma of it, then she closed her eyes to totally absorb the moment.

Before long, there was a frightening knock on her door, which broke the silence, and her wonderful thoughts of Bob. She hopped up, and strolled to the door, still in a daze, but carrying her rose close to her heart, and she peaked through the peephole, to find the porter standing there. She smiled, slipped on her robe and quickly opened the door. Once again, she strolled to the edge of her bed, like a schoolgirl in love, and she pointed to the other side of the room. "Over there, please." And the porter quickly brought her luggage in, collected his tip, and quietly left the room.

She realized, there was to be a short meeting, of sorts, tonight, so she returned her beautiful rose to its vase, and began hanging her clothes in the closet provided. As soon as everything was put away, she turned the shower on, and reached for her rose, and she set it on the vanity, and seductively undressed in front of it. Then she sniffed her rose one last time, and disappeared into the shower.

When she finished drying off, she stood nude in front of her clothing to pick out the perfect dress, for her initial meeting with Mr. Morrison. She picked out a black silky cocktail dress, which she and Sally had bought at Carmella's. While she wiggled into it, she remembered how much fun they'd had that afternoon, buying her new wardrobe. When she finally finished struggling with the zipper, she turned around, for a glimpse of herself, in the mirror. A smile ran across her face. Perfect, she thought. I look red hot in this dress. Sally would be proud, and it makes me feel so sensual, and she strutted in from of the mirror, for a moment, to enjoy the feeling.

Before long, the phone rang, and she elegantly strolled toward it, as if to practice her entrance for Mr. Morrison. "Tina Hargrove. Hello, Mr. Morrison, fifteen minutes, in the lounge, will be perfect. I'll see you then. Bye-bye."

Mr. Morrison's voice sounded very strong, and businesslike. He was very direct, and to the point, she thought, and as she listened to his voice, she sensed no humor what-so-ever, and now, instead of being anxious to meet him, she became apprehensive.

Tina hurried to complete her preparation, for her meeting. The tension began to mount, as she whisked her long black silky hair, behind her shoulders, and she stepped back for one final look at herself. She took a deep breath, and fixed a devilish smile on her face. They'll eat it up, she thought, and then she grabbed her handbag, and made her way to the elevator, for the long ride down.

When she stood in front of the lounge, her anticipation was high, and her heart was pounding, then she took another breath, and entered. The hostess greeted her. "One?" "No, I'm meeting Samuel Morrison." "Okay, this way please." While Tina followed the hostess, her eyes scanned the crowded lounge, looking for whom she thought might be Mr. Morrison. Then, there he was, and he smiled and stood, to greet her.

He was nothing like she had imagined. He was short and a little heavy set, but he had a very distinguished appearance. His freshly cut silver hair highlighted his tan face, and his smile was like a magnet, which drew people to him. He seemed stern, and worldly, but at the same time, humble. He never took his eyes from hers, as she approached, and he kissed her hand, ever so gently, and as he did, he stared with his dark piercing eyes, the entire time. As his lips moved from her hand, a glow surrounded his face, which was etched with character, and he spoke. "Good evening Ms. Hargrove, how was your trip?" "Just wonderful Mr. Morrison, thank you." Then he turned to the woman seated next to him. "I'd like for you to meet my beautiful wife, Emily."

Tina was taken by surprise. This was nothing like she had imagined, and she smiled, and nodded. "Hello Emily, I'm so glad to meet you." The waiter stopped by to help Tina with her chair, and she and Mr. Morrison were seated.

"Well, Ms. Hargrove, how's the weather in Texas, my dear," Emily asked. Tina waved her hand in front of her face, as if to fan herself. "I'm afraid it's very hot," she answered. "This time of the year?" questioned Mr.

Morrison. "Oh yes, it's already in the nineties, and has been for several weeks now." Mr. Morrison stared at Emily. "I'm glad we live in Boston," he playfully remarked. "Aren't you dear?" "Oh goodness yes," she replied. "The temperatures here, hardly ever reach ninety, maybe once or twice a year."

Mr. Morrison seemed very loose, and relaxed, Emily, on the other hand, seemed fidgety, and anxious to leave. Tina could see the strong bond they held, but she realized Emily was an upper class lady. A snobby type, one who was used to being spoiled by her husband, and he was more than happy to oblige.

"Mrs. Morrison and I will not be staying for this meeting tonight. Our son Jonathan will be joining us momentarily, and he will outline the week for you, if that's satisfactory." "That will be fine, Mr. Morrison." "Emily and I wanted to drive up, and meet with you tonight, and then I'll be spending several hours with you in the morning." "Oh, you don't live in Boston?" "Not exactly, we have an estate, thirty-five miles from here. A country estate, of sorts." "Well, I certainly appreciate your driving so far, and so late, just to meet with me." "Well, I know its nerve racking, being in an unfamiliar town, filled with strangers. We felt, we needed to break the ice, if you know what I mean." "That was nice of you, and again, I appreciate it."

Just then, a pleasant expression run across his face, as he looked toward the entrance, and noticed his son. "There's Jonathan now," and he stood, and raised his hand, so Jonathan could see him. It was easy to see, by the twinkle in his eye, the affection he had for his son, as he anxiously awaited his presences. They shook hands, and Jonathan apologized for being late, then he looked across the table, at Emily. "Hello mother. You look divine, as usual." Seemingly, expecting him to make that comment, she thanked him, and turned her face toward the crowd.

Mr. Morrison turned toward Tina, and smiled. "Jonathan, this is Tina Hargrove." Jonathan quickly turned toward her, and his entire expression changed. He seemed star struck, by her beauty. The light shown on Tina's bare shoulders, and the reflection from her silky black dress highlighted her gorgeous smile, and those luscious lips of hers. Her eyes glowed, as she glanced at him, and she reached her hand to him, hoping his luring lips would caress it, and she wasn't disappointed. Jonathan was a tall, slim man, and he carried himself with a touch of dignity, and Tina was immediately overtaken by his magnetic personality.

When he gently took her hand into his, she gazed into his deep eyes, which engulfed hers immediately, and she was swept away by his facial features, as they stood out in the darkly lit room. His smile was captivating, and his lips inviting, and his mustache gave him a distinguished appearance, one which Tina adored. The light shown on his golden blond hair, and as his lust for her beauty prevailed, the excitement danced across his face.

Jonathan gently took her hand, and caressed it with both of his, and he brought it to his lips, and he softly kissed it. She felt the warmth of his hot lips, and electricity shot through her body, which made her want for more. Their eyes never parted, as he slowly rose from the kiss, and he softly spoke. "Tina. What a wonderful name." Then he returned his lips for another taste of her delicious hand, and soon, it was over, and he stood, but he continued to hold her hand.

She was breathless, and taken away from the sheer tenderness of the moment, that she had forgotten where she was. This man had lit a fire in her, one she hadn't realized was there, and as she was brought back to reality, she uttered something foolish, "Nice to meet you sir." Jonathan laughed hard, at her remarks, and everyone joined in. Tina led the parade, however, and her laughter rang out above all the others, not believing what she had just said. "I'm sorry Jonathan." And she giggled. "I'm actually thrilled to meet you." Then she gave his hand a little squeeze, and the laughter died down, and he slithered into a chair next to her.

Mr. Morrison continued to stand, as he made his announcement. "I'm sorry kids, but we have got to run now. It's getting too late for us old folks, and we have a long journey home." Emily rose, and Mr. Morrison moved to her side to help with her chair, then everyone said their goodnights, and in an instant, they were gone.

When Jonathan was seated, Tina shrugged her shoulders, and like two little children, they both giggled, and were glad the old folks were gone. They sat silently for a moment, gazing into each other's eyes, and taking in each other's features, then Jonathan motioned for the waitress, and as he waited, his eyes returned to hers.

"Yes sir." The waitress interrupted. Jonathan's eyes never left Tina's, as he said. "We would like a smaller table please." Then he rose, and moved behind Tina's chair, to pull it out for her, and the waitress said. "Gladly sir, how about over there?" Jonathan had his hand flat on the back of Tina's dress, just below her soft skin, and he pointed to a small, inconspicuous table, in a dark corner of the lounge. "How about that one, over there, Jonathan asked?" "Fine," the waitress agreed, and they followed her to their little hideaway.

As they were seated, their eyes never lost contact, and Tina realized she had never been attracted to anyone, this quickly. She was hopelessly drawn to Jonathan, and his magnetic personality, was overwhelming. Suddenly, the silence was broken. "Tina? It's all right if I call you Tina, isn't it?" She closed her eyes, and didn't say a word, and she slowly nodded her head yes, and then she opened them, and waited to hear what he had to say.

"Tina?" And there was a long silence. "I don't know what to say, exactly," he said, with a soft broken voice, almost as if this powerful man was embarrassed. Her beauty had brought him to his knees, and she knew it, and the words were hard for him to find. She put her hand on his, and patted it. "Don't Jonathan. This is no time for words. I feel it too, so let's order a glass of wine, and enjoy it." Jonathan smiled from relief, and he motioned for the waitress, and his eyes scanned her body.

After he ordered a bottle of wine, it seemed as though no time had passed before the waitress was popping the cork, to break the silence. Jonathan poured a glass for each of them, and neither stopped staring, while he did.

During the second glass, quiet intimate laughter surrounded the table, and simple conversation became very easy, and they had many things in common. As they laughed and talked the night away, each would occasionally touch the other's hand, or hold it, and caress it, and on a couple of instances, Jonathan kissed hers, which sent her into orbit.

Time had seemingly stood still for them, until the waitress came to their table for last call. With a surprised look, each of them glanced at their watches, to find it was one a.m. "My goodness." Tina squealed. "I can't believe it!" They both stood, and quickly walked to the counter, where Jonathan signed the tab, and they made their way to the elevator. Jonathan rode up the elevator with her, and he put his arm around her, and pulled her close to his side, and when he did, she loved it, and she snuggled even closer.

Before they knew it, the doors opened, and after a few short steps, Tina was home. She gazed deeply into his eyes, and he pulled her close to him, and smiled, as he said "Quite an evening." "Quite," she replied. Then she slid her key out of her handbag, and unlocked the door, and he quickly spun her around, into his arms, and his hot lips melted her in the very spot she stood. For several minutes they passionately kissed, and they caressed each other's hot bodies, and at times, they become carried away, as they tugged at each other's clothing wildly, wanting to rip them off.

"Oh Jonathan," and she pulled away, and gasped for air. "You are too much." Jonathan's face was flush, and he also had to catch his breath, but he didn't utter a word, and they both tried to gather themselves. She leaned against the doorway, with the door half opened, and she inhaled deeply, then she exhaled. She gazed into his eyes, then she smiled, and patted his chest, and she mumbled. "You taste so good, and you feel even better. That's why I've got to go." He smiled, and nodded. "I understand."

She lowered her head, and glanced at him, as if she were looking over the top of reading glasses. "Will I see you tomorrow?" He placed a devilish little smile on his face, and replied. "Nothing could keep me away from the office tomorrow." Her eyes lit up, hearing those words, and in a soft seductive voice, she replied. "I can hardly wait." Then she winked at him, and slid through the doorway, and gently closed the door behind her.

Still in a trance, and not believing the evening she had experienced, she kicked her shoes off, and began sliding out of her cocktail dress, and she strolled through the room, on cloud nine.

She tossed her dress on a sitting chair, and fell into her soft bed, and she was lost in thoughts of Jonathan, who was the unexpected thrill of the trip. He had sucked, and bitten her lips so hard, they were numb, but she enjoyed the feeling, and she wished that he were with her now, to finish the job. She slid her hands between her legs, and curled up into a ball, then she noticed how wet her panties were, from the hot passionate events, which had taken place, only a few short minutes ago. She tore them off her hot body, and flung them across the room, and began laughing out loud.

Jonathan, I've never in my life felt such passion. I hardly know you, so it must be lust. Wild, fiery lust, and I love the way lust feels, and she stretched out on the bed, spread eagle.

She closed her eyes, and the events of the hot exciting evening raced through her mind, and she tried to suspend the feelings she had but she could not.

Suddenly, the aroma of the flowers in the room attracted her attention, and she quickly reached for her rose, and she nestled it between her warm breasts, and she was swept away with thoughts of Bob. Then she noticed the message light on her phone was flashing, and she sat on the edge of her bed, and retrieved the message. It was Bob. Damn it! It's too late to return his call now. Maybe I can reach him in the morning, she thought.

She stood, and pulled the covers back, and then she carried her rose to the vanity, where she began to brush her teeth, and she stared into the mirror, at her eyes. With her tooth brush hanging out of her mouth, she stopped brushing, and she braced both of her hands on the vanity for support, and she began thinking of Bob. She pulled the toothbrush from her mouth, and took her rose into her hands, and smelled it's wonderful aroma, and said, "You're not making this decision any easier, Mr. Bob Evans. Not one little bit."

She carried her rose to the balcony door, and pulled the curtain back, and she was overwhelmed by the beautiful view of Boston, and she was torn between thoughts of Jonathan, and then those of Bob. Tina smiled, as she thought, sorry Jonathan, you lose. She strolled to her bed, realizing it was 2a.m., and knowing that she had an early morning meeting. She turned the light out, kissed her rose, placed it back into the vase, slid between the cool silky sheets, and quickly drifted off to sleep.

CHAPTER 10

The Passion of Business

Six a.m. came far too early for Tina, and while her room-coffee-maker did its job, she tried her best to keep her eyes open. Today was a very important day for her. While the other departments of Burgers Inc. had done their jobs selling Mr. Morrison, now it was her turn, to close the deal, by dazzling him with advertising strategies, techniques, and other proven methods, for success. As large as Burgers Inc. had become, the Boston area had virtually been untouched by this burger giant, and Mr. Morrison was a key player in the new growth for the area.

If Tina were to tie down this particular deal, it could mean as many as fifty new restaurants for her company, which may translate to more than $100,000 worth of additional revenue each month, or $1.2 million each year. Tina realized the seriousness, and the importance of the next few days, as she ran her approach, to the situation, through her mind. Tina had basically decided that Burgers Inc. would sell itself, and her real mission was to show Mr. Morrison, and his group, one of the reasons why. Strong marketing!

Mr. Ballard was convinced, through his many meetings with this group, that Mr. Morrison was the very man, who was strong enough to lay the proper foundation, to insure success in the Boston area. Mr. Ballard had done extensive research, and investigations of Mr. Morrison's past business dealings. Mr. Ballard was thoroughly pleased with Mr. Morrison's organizational skills, and his ability to delegate authority and that is what makes Morrison's company a perfect candidate.

Tina was confused, by Jonathan's role with the company, but she did notice Mr. Morrison's smooth approach to business. While he was involved with last night's meeting, to a certain degree, his basic policy seemed to be, let your people have a free hand, simply oversee, pay attention, and direct. Tina admired those qualities in him, and she felt certain, he handled his entire staff, and vast companies, in the same manner.

While Tina huddled over her cup of coffee, her eyes were drawn to the single rose, sitting in the glass vase, on the night stand, next to the bed, and suddenly, she remembered Bob's message last night. She quickly made her way to the phone, and she waited for the operator to answer while she sniffed the beautiful flower. "Yes. This is Tina Hargrove, in room fourteen-twenty-one. I need to place a long distance call to Houston, Texas please."

Tina hoped she could catch Bob this morning, and she sat on the edge of the bed, and counted the rings. Before long, the operator interrupted her thoughts. "I'm sorry. There is no answer." Damn it! She thought. "Could I leave a message please? This is Tina Hargrove, returning his call. Thank you." Tina slammed the phone down, not believing she had missed Bob, and then she smelled his rose one more time, before moving to her closet to pick out her outfit for the day.

When she wiggled her lean body, into the beautiful dress she and Sally had picked out, thoughts of the past few weeks crossed her mind. It had been an emotional roller coaster for her, and she thought of Sally and her actions, and of their conversation. The unique passion Sally brought out in Tina was hot and exciting, but Tina realized she would never forget the sad look on Sally's face, when she told her; she could not be her lover.

Then, there was sweet Bob, and his bon voyage dinner. His surprising statement that he had loved Tina since day one, and that he would wait fifteen more years, if need be. There were his peak-a-boo games in the car, which were extremely exciting, their romantic and sensual dance, his kindness, his gentleness, his thoughtfulness, and his undying love for her. Finally, there were his roses, at the restaurant, and at the hotel.

Then her mind wandered to Jonathan, with his wild and passionate lips, his exciting manner, and the lust they felt for one another, as they almost ripped each other's clothing off, in the hallway, outside her door last night. Tina had never experienced wild passion of that sort before, and she craved that feeling again. I desperately crave it, she thought, and she could imagine his electrifying touch.

She was confused, while she thought of each of those relationships, all unique, and all thrilling. When she gazed into the mirror, a smile of excitement ran across her face, as she realized the many changes her mind and body had been through. She was proud that she had learned to allow herself the freedom to fantasize, and was only confused because the feelings she had were new and exciting. While she didn't have any clear-cut-answers for those feelings, she decided to indulge in all three. Why not? She thought. It's all very exciting and I need to allow myself to act on these fantasies, as well.

She was suddenly startled by the ringing of the phone, and she jumped as though she had been caught doing something wrong. She gave herself a funny stare, in the mirror, and made her way to the phone, where she cheerfully answered. "Good morning. Oh, hi Eric, I've been waiting for you. I'll be right down. Bye-bye." It's big Eric, the limousine driver, she thought, then she quickly gathered her briefcase, and materials for the meeting, and she dashed for the elevator.

When the elevator door opened, to the lobby, Eric was waiting for her, and he led her to the limousine, where they were quickly whisked away in the early morning traffic. It was simply a beautiful morning. The sun was just peeking out from behind a tall building and the air was cool and crisp. It was a nice feeling as Tina watched the city begin to wake from a deep sleep.

Tina continued to glance at her notes, as she prepared for the meeting, but occasionally she glanced up to take in the beauty of Boston. Before long, they arrived in front of the towering office building which housed The Morrison Co., and Eric informed her, the main office was on the tenth floor.

While she stood in the folia and waited for the elevator, she glanced at her watch, and it was seven-forty-five, then she smiled, realizing that she still had fifteen minutes before the meeting, and she relaxed a bit. A crowd gathered, to share her elevator, and when the doors opened, she was herded to the back of it. What a busy place, she thought, and she gasped for what little air they had left her to breathe. Suddenly, she felt a strong fingertip running up her arm, then down again, and she looked around, to see who the hand belonged to, but she couldn't. Then she grabbed the hand, and followed the arm with her eyes, to the shoulder, and then to the face of Jonathan Morrison.

She giggled, and placed her hand flat on her chest, as if to catch her breath, and she was relieved it wasn't someone perverted. "Jonathan, you startled me." Then Jonathan wiggled his way through the mass of bodies, so that he stood next to her, and he softly whispered. "I'm sorry, but I just couldn't resist. That arm of yours looked as though it needed immediate attention."

Tina laughed, and Jonathan giggled. "Jonathan, that's not the only thing which needs attention, believe me." Then they joined hands, and held them to their sides, and he leaned toward her, and kissed her cheek, then he whispered. "I didn't sleep five minutes last night." She smiled, "Poor baby, maybe you'll do better tonight." "I certainly hope not," he quickly replied. Then the elevator door slid open, and she glanced to see the floor number. "Well, we're home Jonathan, it's the tenth floor," and they wiggled, and fought their way through the crowd, and into the hallway.

As they walked down the hallway they were not holding hands, but both of them could feel the fire, which was generated by their passion. And neither of them spoke a word, as they enjoyed each step, and they seemed to bask in the pleasure of being next to one another. She was surprised, at how nothing had changed during the night. The explosive feelings were still there, and she wished she could have ripped his clothing off in the elevator, and she wondered if he was thinking the same thing. Then their hands brushed, as they walked, and she felt the excitement radiating from his body, and they quickly turned to glance into each other's eyes, then they looked straight ahead once again.

Suddenly, the silence was broken. "Here we are Ms. Hargrove," Jonathan said, as he opened the massive, oak door to The Morrison Co. It seemed strange, but exciting to hear him say Ms. Hargrove, she thought. Then she felt like a schoolgirl, who was sneaking around, and she realized that they actually were sneaking around, but she wished that she could taste his lips before they entered the huge board room, to begin their meeting. But, before she knew it, there she was, seated at a long table, filled with employees belonging to Mr. Samuel Morrison. They had been called there, for one reason, and that was to hear what Tina had to say.

From the tenth floor window, the view of Boston was breathtaking. Tina remembered the intimidation of Mr. Ballard's office, but it paled in comparison to this elegant boardroom. Then, Mr. Samuel Morrison entered the room, and with respect, a silence fell over the room. He was smiling, and seemed excited, and he nodded to his employees, as he made his way to the head of the table. While he did, Jonathan was seated at the other end of the table, facing his father, and he smiled at her, and nodded, but everyone's eyes were fixed on Samuel Morrison, in anticipation of his instructions.

Suddenly, he spoke. "Good morning gentlemen." Then, he glanced at Tina, and smiled, and nodded his head. "And lady." Tina blushed, and smiled. Then he continued. "I would like to introduce Ms. Tina Hargrove." Mr. Morrison made a gesture with his hand, as if to point her out, and Tina smiled, and nodded, in recognition.

"As you know, she is from Dallas, Texas, and she represents Burgers Inc. Ms. Hargrove will be with us for a few days, explaining the marketing procedures of her company, and we should take every advantage of this opportunity."

"The Morrison Co.," he continued. "Is on the verge of buying many franchises from Burgers Inc. and I am convinced, to this point, that they are a company, we should associate ourselves with. The only piece of the puzzle, which remains, is their marketing strategies, and Ms. Hargrove will reveal those, to us, this week."

Mr. Morrison stood, and he placed both hands on the table, and leaned forward, and he looked deeply into each set of eyes, one by one, and each of the men sat on the edge of their seats, as they stared at his. "Need I remind you? We will be making our final decision on this matter next week. Therefore, I expect each and every person in this room to take full advantage of Ms. Hargrove's knowledge, and expertise the next few days. Does everyone understand?"

Mr. Morrison stood straight and tall, and he threw his chest out, as a gesture of pride, and everyone could be heard saying "Yes sir," or "Yes Mr. Morrison." And as this went on, Mr. Morrison straightened his jacket, and he smiled as he asked, "Are there any questions?" Mr. Morrison stood waiting for a question, but there were none. "All right then, I'll turn this meeting over to Jonathan, and excuse myself, so you might get some work done. Good luck."

With that, Jonathan rose to his feet, and Mr. Morrison smiled and nodded at Tina, then he made his exit from the boardroom.

The room buzzed, with whispers, for a few moments, as the door closed behind Mr. Morrison, and Jonathan didn't interrupt them, he only gazed into Tina's eyes, and occasionally, he smiled at the others, and nodded. Then, he spoke. "Okay gentlemen." And the room was filled with silence once again, while Jonathan spoke. "I'd like to turn this portion of the meeting over to Ms. Hargrove."

With that, Tina stood, and she harbored a blushing smile, as she began her presentation, and Jonathan smiled with pride, as if he had introduced Miss. America, and he eased back into his seat, anticipating the sound of her voice.

"Good morning gentlemen, I'm very excited to be in Boston this week, and especially excited to be here with your company." Jonathan watched, while Tina transformed herself into a stern business woman, and he marveled as she took control of the powerful men before her. "At this particular meeting, she continued, I will give you a brief rundown of my companies marketing strategies, but as you know, most of our work will take place in the field."

Jonathan was over taken by her confidence, as she gained the respect of every person seated at the huge table, and he smiled with admiration while he watched. "Our marketing department is made up of forty-five dedicated men and women, and our only goal, is your success. In order for the company to achieve success, each individual restaurant must succeed, and that is where we place the emphases."

She paused, and the room buzzed once again, then she continued. "Unlike other restaurant chains, ours is interested in each individual restaurant, and that, my friends, is what sets our company apart from the others."

She had them eating out of her hand, as she continued. "While our company has a very strong national advertising campaign," Then Tina paused, and shook her head yes before she continued, "And I'm sure each of you is familiar with it. We also provide very strong regional support, but then, we take that one step further, and provide even stronger local, and then individual support." She glanced at Jonathan, and he winked, and a particular warmth surrounded her.

Then she came to the most important part of her presentation. "While it's critical for our company to advertise, and to promote our products, it's even more important, and more critical for each individual restaurant to deliver this product, to our customers, in a very professional manner. That gentlemen, means strong management. Management which can produce sparkling clean restaurants, cheerful, happy, well-trained employees, and a quality product, time after time.

With that, she pounded her fist on the table, and she had a vicious look in her eyes, as if to drive home the point, that advertising alone wasn't enough. The room became very quiet, and very still and everyone had their eyes trained on Tina while she stood motionless for a moment, then she continued.

"I can't stress this point enough," she iterated. Then she smiled, and changed her tone. "Now, let's dive into the marketing scheme, and I'll walk you through a typical promotion." Jonathan was dazzled, and taken away with her knowledge, and passion for her job. He sat back and enjoyed each movement she made, through the remainder of her presentation and she felt his eyes fixed on her, and she became excited.

Before long, he heard Tina's last words. "Are there any questions?" There were several, and the participants were excited over her presentation, and they had been involved throughout her message. Now, everyone was eager to have their individual questions answered, and she did, with meticulous authority. She had been a big hit, and as they broke for lunch, everyone involved, stopped by to congratulate her, and to shake her hand, then suddenly, Tina and Jonathan were alone.

He remained seated, and his elbows supported his folded hands, with interlaced fingers, as he gazed over them, with a smile. He stared at Tina's every move, until she walked over, and sat on the edge of the table, next to him. Her bare leg touched his elbow, and it looked inviting, as he brought his hands together, and began clapping. "Bravo," he said. And he continued to applaud. Then, she slowly, and deliberately, slid off the table, and he stared at her beautiful legs, and she knew he was excited by them, and that thought excited her. She smiled at him, and began to curtsy, and she said, "Thank you, thank you very much."

Jonathan stood, and he moved next her and he took her into his arms, and hugged her, then he held her at a distance to stare into her warm eyes, and he softly said, "You were wonderful." Tina's seductive smile found itself on her face, and she blushed a bit, then she said. "Why, thanks again, but it was so easy, while your eyes are focused on me."

Then she became uncomfortable, and afraid that someone may walk in, and catch them. She placed her hand flat on his chest, and gently pulled away. "Come on; let's have lunch, before we're caught by someone." Jonathan grabbed her hand, and pulled her back into his arms, for a passionate taste of her hot lips, and she melted, then she pulled him closer. "Oh Jonathan, you're driving me crazy." "And you, me," he quickly replied.

She pulled away again, and walked to the door, and she tried to gather herself. "Not now, Jonathan." Then she glared at him. "And not here!" He gently closed his eyes, and gritted his teeth, and nodded yes, then he joined her, and they left the boardroom, for lunch.

All through lunch, Jonathan's eyes were trained on her, and he had very little to say, he simply stared, in awe of her beauty. She knew he had been aroused by her performance, and she anxiously anticipated raising his level of excitement even higher, during the next few days.

Just as he called the waiter to their table for the check, he turned to her, and asked, "How about dinner tonight? "I'd love to Jonathan. Where are you taking me?" "Oh, I know a swanky little place on the east end, where I'd love, to show you off." She blushed, and replied. "Sounds like fun, and I'll make sure you won't be disappointed." Jonathan stood, and helped Tina to her feet, and then he whispered. "You could never disappoint me." She giggled, and took his hand, and led him from the restaurant. "Come on silly, we've got work to do."

She continued to impress the powerful men of The Samuel Morrison Company, all afternoon, then, she and several of them left to visit various TV and radio stations, leaving Jonathan on his own. At one particular TV station, she realized that Boston was a very expensive market to do business in. Even more so than the Dallas area, and the three men, she had brought along, watched her negotiating skills in action.

By the end of the day, Tina had gotten her foot in the door of a multimillion dollar corporation, and then she negotiated an acceptable deal, with the largest TV station in the area. She was basking in the glory, when they returned to the confines of the boardroom, only to find Jonathan gone for the day. She said her goodbyes to the men whom she had spent the afternoon with, and she glanced at the clock on the wall. It was five-forty-five, and she wondered what time to expect Jonathan, while she stood all alone in the boardroom. Then she smiled, and her eyes roamed the room and she turned and strolled toward the elevator to make her way back to the hotel.

Once she was in her room, she kicked her shoes off, and slipped out of her dress, and then she eased into the sitting chair, overlooking Boston. She was thrilled at how the business end of the day had gone, but she wondered where Jonathan was, and why she hadn't heard from him. Then she drifted off to sleep.

Forty-five minutes later, she was startled, by a loud knock on her door. She jumped up from her chair, trying to reorient herself, and rubbing the sleep from her eyes, and then she slipped her robe on, and noticed the clock was glaring, seven o'clock. "Oh my goodness, I can't believe I fell asleep."

When she opened the door, she found the bellboy, with a note from Jonathan, and as she closed the door, she ripped the envelope open. "Something came up, and I'll have to give you a rain check on dinner, but I would love to meet you later for a drink. I have wonderful news. I'll call you. Jonathan."

She leaned against the door, with disappointment, and her fantasy of a night on the town with Jonathan, withered away. She dragged herself toward the bed, where she sat on the edge of it in disgust, and she ripped the note into little pieces, and threw it into the air. "Damn it!" she thought. "Then a smile ran across her face, as she realized that surely, he felt the same as her, and whatever the reason he canceled, it must have been important. He'll call later, she thought, and I'll be ready.

Just then, her phone rang, and she rushed over to answer it, thinking it may be Jonathan. "Hello," she said excitedly. "Oh, hi Bob." Tina was surprised to hear Bob's voice, and she rested her hand flat against her forehead, hoping he didn't pick up on that. "It's so good to hear your voice. I miss you too darling. And Bob, the roses were simply perfect. In fact, I'm smelling one of them right now." She brought it to her nose, and sniffed it. "You'll never know what they meant to me. Thank you so much. What time did you get home today? Four-thirty, oh that's very early."

"I'm sorry I missed you yesterday, did you get my message? No, when you called, I was at a meeting, and I didn't get your message until it was too late to call back. I know it's never too late, but I didn't want to wake you. You probably needed your beauty sleep." Then she giggled.

Bob asked how her trip was going. "Oh honey, just great. We had our first meeting this morning, and I don't think they've gotten over it yet," and she and Bob laughed. "But I have a meeting later on this evening, and apparently there's good news coming. No, I don't know what the news is; only that it's supposed to be good. God darling, I miss you too, and I can't wait for Thursday. You're still going to pick me up, aren't you? Great. I love you too, and I'm so glad you called. Bye Bob, I'll call you tomorrow.

When she hung up the phone, she fell back into her bed, and she caressed the rose between her breasts. He is such a nice man, she thought, then she smelled it again, and reminisced of their dinner Friday night, and the exciting evening they'd had. A warm feeling ran through her body, and she could visualize his arms holding her tight, and how secure she felt. She remembered his soft gentle kisses, and his confident manner, but more important, she remembered his uncanny patience with her, and their entire relationship. How anyone could love another person for fifteen years, and be silent about it all that time, is unbelievable she thought.

She was embarrassed by the many times, in the past, that she had asked his advice, concerning her other relationships, and how unselfish he was, and how he was constantly there for her, but he never gave a hint that he was in love with her. He'd hoped that one day, she would finally notice, and fall in love with him, just as he had with her.

While she loved Bob, she craved Jonathan, and his fiery manner, and her thoughts were torn between the two. Then she realized, for the time being, she was in

Boston, and she fully intended to pursue those lustful feelings, and experience the passion at hand. Jonathan had given her something new. A fiery passion she had never felt before, and she couldn't help herself. She drooled at the very thought of them ripping each other's clothing from their hot and exciting bodies and she had decided to do just that.

Jonathan finally called, at ten-thirty, and Tina was working on material for tomorrow's meeting. The ring of the phone sounded urgent, and she rushed over to answer it quickly. "Hello. Oh, hi Jonathan. No, I'm not angry, just very disappointed. You've been at your father's all evening? Why won't you tell me now? Okay, I'll meet you in the lounge at eleven-thirty. I can't wait to see you either. Bye-bye."

She hung the phone up, and she was excited, but confused. He had exciting news from his father, but he wouldn't share it with her over the phone. She couldn't be bothered with that now. Time was short, and she had to pick out a seductive dress for Jonathan, and get herself ready before eleven-thirty.

She left her room at eleven-thirty and during the elevator ride she wondered what in the world Jonathan had to say and she anticipated the excitement. Finally, the doors slid open and he was waiting in front of the lounge. Her excitement was bubbling over, and he rushed to her side, and took her hand, then he softly kissed her lips. "I'm sorry about dinner, beautiful, but I simply didn't have a chance to call." "That's okay, you're here now, and I'm glad of that." He stared into her eyes as he asked, "Are you really?" She smiled, and sheepishly nodded her head yes.

While they strolled to the entrance of the lounge, Jonathan whispered, "I can't wait to tell you the news." She stopped, and spoke. "Well, tell me now, silly." He took her hand, and led her into the lounge. "Be patient, I will, I will."

While they were escorted through the lounge, her imagination ran wild. What news could he possibly have, that would be this exciting? Was it business related? Was it personal? Did it have anything to do with me? She thought.

Finally, they were seated, and Jonathan ordered drinks, then he took Tina's hand in his, and his eyes were twinkling. Tina glared at him, and shook his hand back and forth. "Well?" He stared deeply into her eyes, as if he were preparing to savor her reaction. "I have good news, and better news." Then there was silence.

"Come on Jonathan, spit it out." He giggled. "Okay, okay. We've made our decision to get involved with Burgers Inc." Disappointment ran across Tina's face. Despite the fact that it was good, business news, she really expected much more. "And that's it?" she questioned. "No. Actually, there's more." She raised her hands, and began to rotate them in a circle, as if to say, go on.

"Well, my father has received reports on your performance all day, and simply based on those reports, he . . . . We have decided to follow through, and buy the franchise rights to the entire Boston area. Therefore, we'll have a short meeting in the morning at nine a.m., and the rest will be canceled, and he and I, will fly to Dallas next week to sign the papers.

She was devastated, by the news. "Canceled?" And Jonathan became puzzled, when he saw the sadness in her eyes. "What's wrong darling, I thought you'd be thrilled?" "Well, I am, but . . . I was just getting to know you." His expression turned serious, as he said. "Honey, can't you see? This means we'll be working together. A lot." Then he raised his eyebrows, as if to persuade her to agree.

Suddenly, the waitress interrupted, with the wine, and Tina fixed her eyes on Jonathan's, realizing her entire plan for hot sex this week was in jeopardy. Tina smiled, and she excused herself, and she slowly walked to the ladies' room, where she slammed her hands on the vanity, and stared into the mirror. "Damn it!" she yelled. And as she continued to stare at herself, in the mirror, she thought, I'm not going to let this happen! She quickly brushed her hair back, and gathered herself, and then she marched back to the table, as if she were on a mission.

Jonathan had a puzzled expression on his face, while he watched her return, and he could see the fire in her eyes, as she approached him. She snatched the bottle of wine from the table, and took Jonathan's hand, and bellowed, "Come with me!" He was overwhelmed, as she pulled him through the lounge, and to the elevator, but not a word was spoken.

Once the elevator door opened, she pushed him into the very back of it, and she stood in front of him, as if to guard him, while she waited for the door to close. He laughed, and asked. "What is this?" She glared at him, and she slowly walked toward him, in a very catlike way. She placed both hands flat on his chest, and softly said. "Jonathan, I want you." Then she slowly began unbuttoning his shirt, and he aggressively wrapped his arm around her waist, and pulled her body against his. "I want you too," he whispered. Then he nibbled on her ear.

She was on fire, when she heard the ringing of a bell, and the elevator door opened. She grabbed his belt, and held it tight, with her hand, and she pulled him out of the elevator, and toward her room. In front of her door, she stopped, and slid into his arms, and their lips met, and she lost control, and she began pulling his shirt from his pants. She wanted him more than she had ever wanted anything before.

As they kissed, she handed him the key, and he unlocked the door, but their lips never parted, and once it opened, they fell into the room, and she kicked the door closed. Jonathan was overcome with passion, and he wanted her, every bit as much as she wanted him. He tugged at her beautiful dress, then his hand made its way to the zipper, and his hand rubbed against her soft skin, as he peeled the dress away.

In her excitement, she wildly, pulled his shirt apart at the buttons and she pushed it to his shoulders, then she kissed his chest, and quickly moved her hands to his belt, to unfasten it. She wrapped her hands around his body, and squeezed his butt with her hands, and pulled his body next to hers, and she felt his sweat, as their bodies met. Jonathan slid her dress to the floor, and she grabbed the zipper of his pants, and quickly peeled them to the side, and her hands slithered down the back of them, and they fell to the floor.

He took her hot luscious lips with his teeth as they moved away from their clothing, to the edge of the bed, where he wildly tossed her slender body into it, then he stepped out of his briefs, and socks. She held her hands out for him, and her face was flush, and her eyes seemed dazed, then he melted against her hot body, and she was swept away, while he savagely kissed her neck, then down to her breasts, then to her lips once again.

She dug her finger nails into his back, and pulled him tighter into her body, until she could feel every curve of it, and him hers. And they exploded from the passion until exhaustion set in and they collapsed next to one another.

Tina was ravished, and had never felt as hot as she did at that very moment, and she threw her arm around him, and she pulled him closer, while they caught their breath.

He was sweating, and breathing hard, and it drove her wild. She could never have imagined love making being so wild, and the simple pleasure of it caused her to thirst for more. It was a new experience for her and her eyes glistened, in the dimly lit room, while she clutched his sweating body and they drifted off to sleep.

CHAPTER 11

Betrayal

When her eyes opened, the next morning, she was exhilarated, and her body ached from the passion of last night. It had been a long time, but never had she experienced those feelings. The hot passion, they shared, was fresh on her mind, and after reliving the wild and lustful love making, she and Jonathan shared, she quickly rolled over, to find him gone. On the pillow was a note.

"Sorry, I had to leave so early. Last night was nice. Hope you slept well. See you soon. Jonathan."

Nice! She thought. Nice? What a cold note, and what the hell does he mean by, see you soon? Why couldn't he have said, I can't wait to see you again, or even have hung around for an encore? But no, instead, he says last night was nice, and I'll see you soon.

She was furious, and decided to call him, and find out exactly what the meaning of his note was, and why he left without a word. She called his home, and a woman answered. "Morrison's resident." Tina was very surprised to hear a woman's voice.

"Hello, this is Tina Hargrove, could I speak with Jonathan please?" "Who is this, again?" she asked. "Tina Hargrove, with Burgers Inc." "No, I'm sorry. My husband is running an errand." Husband? She thought, and she almost fell out, when she heard that awful word.

Married! . . And she became nervous, and she couldn't wait to get off the phone. "I'm sorry to bother you at home. I'll try him at the office." "I'm afraid he won't be in the office today. We're going on a retreat this morning." "Okay, I'm sorry to bother you, bye-bye."

Married! She screamed, as she hung up. You sorry bastard! Why didn't you tell me? Then she tried to justify. I didn't ask, but he didn't. . . . You son-of-a-bitch! God I feel so damned stupid. She snatched his note from the table, and wadded it up, and threw it across the room, and then she stormed to her luggage, and began stuffing her clothing into them, thinking, I've got to get the hell out of this place.

Tears were streaming down her face, and she grabbed her beautiful new dresses from their hangers, and crammed them into the bags. When one was full, she flung the bag across the room, and filled another one. After each bag was full, they lay in a pile, next to the door, and Tina laid face down, crying into a pillow. She grabbed the other pillow, and threw it across the room, and it knocked a lamp to the floor. How could I be so damned ignorant? Shit! You bastard!

She glanced at the clock, and it was seven-thirty, and she decided to get dressed, and get the hell out of her room. By eight-ten, she was dressed, and the bellboy was carrying her luggage to the elevator. When the doors closed, he asked, "Ma'am is everything okay?" "Hell no!" she snapped. "But everything will be just fine very soon, in fact, just as soon as I get out of Boston!"
Not another word was spoken, until the doors opened, and when she walked past him, she stopped, and rested her hand on his shoulder, "Listen. I'm sorry. I've

just had a lousy morning. "I understand," he replied, "Don't worry about it."

She stormed to the counter and checked out of the hotel, and then she sat in a chair, in the lobby. As she waited for her limousine, she realized that this would be her last meeting with The Morrison Company for this trip. Her emotions were jumbled, and tears glazed her eyes, and she knew she had to pull herself together, but she couldn't.

Tina realized it didn't matter, what Jonathan had done, he was only one man. Unfortunately for him, he was a dishonest son-of-a-bitch, but at least she had successfully closed the business deal for her company, and that's what really mattered.

She was disgusted and almost sick while she watched strangers laugh, and giggle, and enjoy one another, as they entered the hotel lobby. Some were cuddling, and some were caressing one another, and some were holding hands, but they all seemed happy, except for her. She seemed out of place, in a room where everyone expressed love, and she felt hate. While she knew, she was the one who dragged Jonathan to her room, she also knew he didn't resist, or give any hint of being married. She hated him for that, and then she hated herself for being so damn foolish.

Her tears were all but gone, when Eric drove up, and she decided to put thoughts of Jonathan in the past, where they belonged. While Eric walked through the doors, she stood next to her luggage, and waved to him.

She was a pitiful sight. Her hair wasn't brushed, and her makeup had been thrown on, and he could tell she had been crying. She looked like a sad puppy, someone had disowned, and Eric asked, "Ms. Hargrove, what happened? And why are you standing in the lobby with your luggage?" "Nothing happened Eric, but I'm going home where I belong, right after my meeting. Come on, let's get this shit in the car, and you can take me to the office."

She spent the entire trip with her face buried in the mirror, trying to hide her sorrow, and anger, and then, they were there. "Eric, don't get out," she snapped, "I'll get the door myself. Could you please pick me up at noon, and drive me to the airport?" "Yes Ms. Hargrove, I certainly will, and I. . . ." "Don't say it, Eric. I'll be just fine. Don't worry about me, bye for now." "Good luck Ms. Hargrove."

While Tina stood before the towering building, she remembered the feeling she had, when she first arrived in Boston, and stood in this very spot. The excitement and high expectations she had then, were now replaced with sadness. An urgency to leave this town, had overtaken her, and while she made her way to the elevator, she hoped Mr. Morrison wouldn't notice.

When she entered the boardroom the twelve men were already seated, and they turned their heads toward her, and smiled. One of them blurted out, "Good morning Tina, how are you feeling today?" She smiled, and wanted to tell the poor soul she felt awful and that she felt betrayed, by the very man, that he worked for. She wanted to tell this man how Jonathan had torn her heart out, and lied to her, and taken advantage of her, then simply left her to lick her own wounds. But she didn't. Instead, she transformed herself into a woman with a bubbly personality, and she responded. "I'm feeling wonderful, and so proud to be here with all of you this morning."

It surprised her, to hear those words spill out of her mouth, but she was happy they had, even though she didn't actually feel that way at all. In reality she didn't want to be there. She wanted to be on a plane headed for Dallas, and to put as much distance, as she could, between her and Boston. Then she was seated, and she smiled, realizing, that soon, she would do just that.

Mr. Samuel Morrison entered the room, and all heads turned toward him, and again a hush fell on everyone's lips, as he did. He seemed excited, and cheerful, and the sight of it, made Tina sick. Why couldn't my fantasy with you have come true she asked herself, instead of one with that lying ass son of yours? And why isn't that lying coward here, anyway?

Mr. Morrison stood behind his chair, while he spoke, "Gentlemen, and lady." He smiled, and nodded toward Tina and everyone laughed. Then he continued "Our meetings with Ms. Hargrove have been outstanding and very productive. Based on reports from you," then he pointed his finger around the table, at each man seated, "We have decided to move forward with our plans to buy the Burgers Inc. franchise for the Boston area." Everyone applauded, and shouted, "Here, here," and Tina lowered her head, and blushed.

"With that in mind," he continued, "We will cut these meetings, with Ms. Hargrove, short, and meet with her again next week in Dallas, where Jonathan and I will consummate the deal. Then my friends, we will be in the burger business." The applause reappeared, and a buzz of excitement filled the room. Tina smiled and nodded, as she glanced into each set of eyes, which were focused on her, and then her eyes were drawn toward Mr. Morrison. He seemed thrilled, and clapped along with everyone else, and as he continued to clap, he moved his hands toward Tina, as if to give her all the credit and he stared deeply into her eyes.

Mr. Morrison finally lifted his hands, to silence the commotion, and to regain control of the meeting, and then once again, he spoke.

"I'm sorry Jonathan couldn't be here for this moment, but he's on a well-deserved vacation. However, he did ask me to read this note to you." Tina sat on the edge of her seat in anticipation of Jonathan's words, but could only think of the hatred she felt for him, and how stupid she felt.

Mr. Morrison turned toward Tina, and read the note. "Tina, you were magnificent, and we are thrilled to become a part of your company. I'm sorry I could not be here today, but am very anxious to see you next week in Dallas."

All sorts of evil thoughts entered her mind, as Mr. Morrison read those pitiful words. You bet I'm magnificent, you coward bastard, but you can bet that you'll be seeing as little of me as I can manage.

Mr. Morrison glanced at his watch, while the room buzzed, then he held his hands up once more, for everyone to quiet down. "Time is running short, and I would love to hear from Ms. Hargrove before we adjourn." With that, Tina gathered her since of humor, and stood before the dazzled group of businessmen, not really knowing what to say. She wasn't in the mood for any of this, and she only wanted to go home. Tina took a deep breath, and began.

"Thank you gentlemen, I'm extremely, overwhelmed by your quick decision, and greatly appreciate your hospitality during my short trip." She paused, and gazed around the room, and remembered her first meeting with this group of men, and how successful it had been. She remembered the feeling she had, while Jonathan's eyes were fixed on her that day, and how excited and hot it made her feel. But now, those feelings were gone, and only hatred remained and then she continued. "I must say I'm thrilled and speechless." Then she moved from her chair and she began slowly pacing around the table, toward Mr. Morrison, and she smiled at him, then to the others.

"I'm very impressed with each of you, and your company, but especially with this man." And she placed her hand on Mr. Morrison's shoulder, and then she continued her stroll around the table. "With your help, he has accomplished what most people only dream of." And as she completed her trip around the table, she stopped at her chair, and wiggled in front of it. "And I must say, "It's great to live in America!"

The applause rang out once again and she moved toward Mr. Morrison and shook his hand. Then he raised her hand to his lips, and gently kissed it, and Tina and Mr. Morrison disappeared through his door.

Behind the door, was Mr. Morrison's impressive office, and while he moved toward his chair, he motioned for her to have a seat. "Well Ms. Hargrove, you've had an exciting couple of days, haven't you?" If he only knew, she thought. "That I have, Mr. Morrison, thanks to you." "No Ms. Hargrove thanks to you. I've been very impressed with your entire company, but when I heard you speak and I heard your opinion. . . . Well, I must say, I was very impressed and relieved."

"Relieved?" she questioned. "Yes, relieved. You see, my company has never seen a project fail, and I understand the restaurant business is very risky. But after meeting with representatives from your company and then finally meeting with you, well, you were the icing on the cake. If everyone at your company is as dedicated as you, and I'm convinced they are. Then Burgers Inc. is a safe bet.

Tina blushed, for a moment, and she put her problems, with Jonathan, aside. She realized the important thing here, was Mr. Morrison, and his company, and Burgers Inc., and the relationship, between the two companies, which had just transpired. She was proud, and thankful, that she had been received so well and she appreciated the confidence Mr. Morrison had shown in her and the company which she represented.

"Well, thank you Mr. Morrison. I'm flattered. And I appreciate you saying that but I can't stand failure either and you can bet I will do my part to see that you succeed." He nodded yes, and smiled as he said, "I believe you will, and I appreciate that." Mr. Morrison glanced at his watch once again. "But, for now, you don't want to miss your flight."

With that Tina stood and they shook hands and then she disappeared through the front door of his office and stood, alone, in the hallway. She sighed from relief as she gathered her thoughts and then she hurried toward the elevator so she could leave this god forsaken place for the safety of her world in Dallas, Texas.

CHAPTER 12

I Hate the Rain

It had been cold on the plane, but the warmth of DFW airport filled the air, and Tina was glad to be home, away from Jonathan Morrison, and his lies. She still kicked herself, for her ignorance, but was glad she was able to experience, the hot passion of last night, for the first time in her life. While she stood motionless, in the crowded airport, she conjured up those feelings and smiled a devilish little smile. She realized how wonderful last night felt and how she would never trade those feeling for anything in the world despite the results.

Then, she was quickly brought back to reality when someone brushed against her and she realized she needed to claim her luggage and then hale a taxi for her short trip home. In her frustration she had not called Bob to let him know she was coming home early, instead, she decided to take a cab and then surprise him later.

She rushed through the terminal, with a smile of happiness, only thinking of getting home to the safety of her own little world. And soon she was in the cab and before long the cab was turning into her beautiful driveway, in front of her beautiful home, where she opened her beautiful front door, and entered her palace.

Tina was thrilled to be home and she held her hands out and she smiled as she turned around and around, and hummed a cheerful little tune. She visited each room of the house, like George Bailey returning to Bedford Falls and saying, hello little kitchen, hello sweet bedroom, hello you snuggly little den, and hello you beautiful deck. It's great to be home, she said.

She glanced at her clock and it was four p.m. Still two hours before Bob would get home from work and she went to her bedroom and flung herself on the bed and she cherished this time alone. She curled herself into a ball and filled her mind with happy thoughts of Bob and of her daddy's upcoming birthday and the victory of success in Boston and how wonderful it was to be alive. Then she knew that Jonathan's actions could not bring her down, or hold her back, or interfere with her life in any way. What happened there would stay there and only be a faint memory, very faint, she thought.

She picked up the phone, and called her mom. "Hello mom. No, I'm not calling from Boston," she giggled. "I'm at home. My meeting was cut short and here I am. I just walked in the door. How's the birthday boy?" and they laughed. "I can't wait till next Monday. I know he's going to love the new boat. What time is Whitney's going to deliver it? Ah, four-thirty. Great, I'll take off from work early and try to get there by four o'clock. It'll be a great surprise." She listened while Joan told her that she had to go. Joan and James were on their way to a dinner club where they were to meet some friends and that she didn't want to be late. "Have fun mom; I'll talk to you later. Bye-bye."

She stood from her bed and danced around the room while she unpacked her luggage and put her things away. When she shook the wrinkles from her beautiful new outfits her thoughts turned to that magical day, last week, when her and Sally picked them out. What a dear friend

Sally is, she thought. We had such a fun time at Carmella's and I hope we can do it again.

She began thinking of her vow, while she was in Boston, to explore a relationship with Sally and then she laughed out loud thinking of Jonathan and all that he had done. She immediately decided that Bob was the man for her and that any exciting relationship with another woman was just that, for other women. She smiled thinking of Bob and all that he meant to her and she shook her head, in disgust, thinking how foolish she had been venturing out with Jonathan.

Suddenly, her attention was diverted to her bedroom window where she noticed rain drops falling against the glass. Soon the drops turned into streams of water like little rivers to the bottom of the window, and then they disappeared from sight as they flowed toward the ground. Tina loved rain but as she sat in the floor watching it, through the glass, there was a flash of lightning and then a crash of thunder.

Oh my, she thought, a Texas thunderstorm! While she loved rain, she certainly did not enjoy storms, or thunder, or lightning. Then, there was another crash of thunder as the storm quickly moved through the area. She stood, and walked toward the window for a closer look and then the lights flickered and another crash of thunder and then the lights went out, and her house became dark. She stood dead in her tracks, hoping the electricity would return quickly, but it didn't. Then her eyes adjusted to the dark and she continued staring out the window. As she looked through the glass, the rain was coming down in sheets, more rain than she had ever seen.

Before long the water in the street rose above the curb and then more lighting, and more thunder, and then silence, and then more heavy rain. Nature was angry and reared her ugly head and the sight was awesome and the rain came down in sheets, almost in waves.

She felt very tiny and vulnerable. Almost like a speck to the earth and she became frightened hoping a tornado wouldn't rip through the neighborhood. Suddenly the violence died down and the lights came back on and she felt safe again. She glanced at her watch and it was five p.m. Gosh, where has the time gone, she thought, then she moved away from the window and at that very moment the phone rang, and it startled her.

She rushed to it, and answered timidly, "Hello." It was Bob's voice. "Tina, I'm glad your home. Listen, something terrible has happened, and I need to see you right now!" Tina had never heard this tone in his voice before. "Bob, how did you know I was home?" "Tina, never mind that, I must see you now! I'll meet you at the 7-11, at the corner of Stemmons and Mockingbird. And Tina, be careful.

She threw a pair of jeans and a flannel shirt on her nude body, and dashed out the door where she wadded through ankle deep water and backed her car into bumper deep water in the street and she drove away. As she did, her tires caused the water to fly above her car and they made huge waves in the street.

The driving was treacherous and she was amazed at the number of cars, on the side of the road, and in ditches. She saw many accidents, and the amount of water on the highways was unbelievable, but finally, the Mockingbird exit was three miles ahead. She noticed the rain begin to fall once again and then it turned into a driving rain and she could barely see the highway and she was forced to pull her car to the side of the road and wait it out.

Soon, the rain stopped and her nerves were getting the best of her. She could only imagine what the urgency was with Bob. His voice sounded desperate and something terrible had happened, he said. What could it be? She thought. But she only knew she had to hurry, and then she'd know.

Before long the 7-11 was in sight, and Tina could see Bob standing out front, in the rain, pacing back and forth, and waiting for her. The traffic was heavy and she had a terrible time crossing the street, but soon, there was a break in it and she hurried across. As Tina made it to the parking lot she locked her brakes, turned the car off and flung open the car door, and rushed to Bob's side.

He was dripping wet but when he saw her he rushed to her side, and took her into his arms. He had been crying, and Tina asked. "Baby, what's the matter?" He squinted his eyes and he looked deeply into hers. "Tina, something terrible has happened." The words were difficult for him and he paused to gather himself. "Bob, what is it, what has happened?"

A gentle expression swept through his face as he opened his mouth and uttered the words. "Tina. I have a good friend who's a policeman. And. . . . He. . . uh, called. Well shit! Tina, it's your parents. They were in an accident." Tina had a puzzled look on her face as she asked. "What did you say?" "Tina, I'm sorry. I'm so sorry, but they've been killed."

Tina was soaked, as the rain continued, and she pulled away from Bob and she screamed. "What kind of sick joke is this buster? I just talked with my mom and you have the audacity to stand there and tell me that they're dead?" She began pounding her fists against his chest. "I hate you, you liar. Why the hell are you doing this to me? What is wrong with you?" Tina suddenly turned and she hurried toward her car. "Tina please!" Bob pleaded. She swung the car door opened as she said, "I'll show you, you bastard, my parents are fine." She slid into the seat, slammed the door, started the car, and sped away, in the driving rain.

Tina had no idea where she was going, as she violently backed the car up, and spun the tires. Then she threw the car into drive and the car fishtailed off the parking lot and onto the highway not paying any attention what-so-ever to the traffic. Fortunately, she didn't hit anyone but tires could be heard screeching and brakes were locked, to avoid her, then she turned the corner and disappeared into the traffic of Interstate 35.

Her thoughts were jumbled while she sped down the highway. Tears streamed down her cheeks and she hit the steering wheel with her fists. Hurry up car! Then she decided to go to the police station. It's impossible, she thought. I just talked to mom. He's wrong; he's made a terrible mistake. Then she began to rationalize. Maybe they were in an accident, and only hurt. Maybe I should go to the hospital. But which one she thought? No, I'll go to the police station.

She drove wildly through the traffic and everyone she passed blew their horn, trying to get her to slow down but she paid them no attention and she continued to weave in and out of the traffic, in the driving rain. Before long, the traffic came to a halt, on the interstate, as she neared downtown Dallas and she quickly pulled toward the shoulder and floored the gas pedal and the car fishtailed passed everyone.

Tina made her exit and she sped through a yellow traffic light, at the bottom of the hill, and she weaved between the cars as she continued on the service road. Then in the distance, she saw the problem. There was an awful accident, involving an eighteen wheeler, and several cars. The truck had been overturned and it blocked the entire highway and then she noticed an off ramp in front of her and a clear interstate. She quickly exited and sped toward Elm Street and the short drive to downtown and finally to the police station.

There were several policemen scampering around, outside the building, when she drove up. She slammed on her brakes, squealed her tires, flung the door opened and dashed inside the building. The officers only stopped and stared but she didn't give a shit. Her only thoughts were to get inside and to find someone, anyone, who would tell her that Bob had lost his mind, and didn't know what the hell he was talking about.

She rushed to the counter soaking wet and out of breath and she pounded on the counter in front of her and she screamed, "Somebody help me!" The entire department looked up and two officers, on her side of the counter, rushed to her side. "Yes ma'am, what's the problem?" I'm Tina Hargrove. I'm looking for my parents. Has anyone seen my parents?" "Ma'am settle down, just settle down." And the officer's tried to walk her across the room to a row of chairs, to seat her, and calm her down. She broke away from them and she rushed back to the counter, and clutched it. "Leave me alone damn it. I've got to find my parents, don't you understand?"

An officer on the other side of the counter came forward and he held her hand while the other two officers joined her from behind, to make sure she didn't begin running wildly through the building. All eyes were glued to them when the officer, who was holding her hand, spoke. "Okay. Now. What's the problem again?" "Are you fucking deaf?" she bellowed. "I've got to find my parents!" And the two officers began to restrain her and to keep her put.

"Ma'am, I want to help you but you are not making any sense. Slow down and tell me the problem and I'll help you." Tears were streaming down Tina's face and she cried out loud then she tried to catch her breath, stop the tears, compose herself and collect her thoughts, but she couldn't. She only heard the voice of an officer saying, "It's okay," while he patted her back like that of a child.

Finally, her voice broke as she said, "My name is. . . . Tina Hargrove. My parents. . . They've. . . ." She cried so hard the words wouldn't come out. "It's okay ma'am. Just take your time." "I've got to find my parents!" she snapped. "Someone told me they were in an accident!"

"What sort of accident?" he asked "Automobile?" "Yes, damn it!" "Okay, just settle down. Now, what are their names?" "James Hargrove and Joan Hargrove. Where the hell are they?" she screamed.

"Now we're getting someplace," he said, while he wrote the names down. "Just one minute, and I'll check."

He moved to a computer, where he began typing furiously. "Hurry! Please hurry." "Ma'am, this may take a few minutes, we've had so many traffic accidents the past hour. Please, let these two officers take you to the next room, for some coffee, and I'll bring you the news as soon as I can."

"I'm not going anyplace!" she yelled. The officer stood and placed his hands on his hips and glared at her, as if to say, if you want this done you had better go with them. She stood back from the counter and held her hands in the air. "Okay, okay, but please hurry!

The officers escorted her to the next room where she was seated at a large table and given a hot cup of coffee. The room appeared to be an interrogation room, one used for criminals, and murders, and thugs, and thieves. She was none of those and she wondered why she was even there at all. One of the officers spoke while the other stared. "It won't be long ma'am; it's just been a busy night with the storm and all." The other officer left the room for a second and then returned with a towel and he handed it to Tina, so that she could dry her hair, and face. She noticed a puddle of water; she had left on the table and she blotted it up.

"What the hell is taking so long? How hard can it be?" Where is that guy?" "Ma'am, believe me, he's working on it as fast as he can." Just then, he entered. And from the gloomy expression on his face, she knew the news wasn't good. She stood, and rushed to his side. "Are they okay, are they alright?" she screamed." He took her hand, but he didn't say a word, while he led her to the table, and continued to hold it, and stretched it over the table, while she was seated on one side, and he on the other.

"Well?" she asked. His eyes were glaring, and serious, and then his lips moved. "Tina, I'm sorry. Your parents are gone." She sat silent and motionless, much to the officer's surprise, but she cried, as she asked. "How?" Then she stared deeply into his eyes, waiting for his answer.

He squeezed her hand. "Tina, it happened during the storm." She closed her eyes, remembering, at that time, she had been staring out the window of her bedroom, watching the streets fill with violent rain, and watching the flashes across the sky, and then listening for the crashes of thunder, and ducking her head, hoping the lightning wouldn't strike her house. A flood of tears rushed through her eyes, and down her cheeks, then she softly opened them, waiting to hear more.

Then, the officer spoke, "The rain was coming down so hard, and the interstate was like a river. They tried to pull to the shoulder, to wait it out, but they didn't see the truck next to them. The truck hit them on the passenger side, and the truck driver hit his breaks as their car was spun around, in front of the truck, where it hit them again, and knocked them down an embankment, and wrapped the car around a light pole, on the service road. They were killed instantly. . . . I'm so sorry Tina."

She broke the tight grip he had on her hand, and she stood, and began pacing back and forth, like a caged animal. "It can't be, it simply can't be." She brought her hands to her face, and cried into them, and the two officers hugged her, and comforted her.

"They can't be dead." she yelled. "They can't be. This is a nightmare. Please, someone, wake me up!" The officers held her tight, not wanting her to do anything foolish, then the door opened, and there stood Bob.

She glanced at him, and rushed to his side, and wrapped her arms around him, and cried out loud. "Oh Bob, they're dead! They're gone. What am I going to do?" The officers filed out of the room, and Bob squeezed her tightly. "Tell me it's not true Bob; please tell me I'm having a nightmare. He held her tighter, and pulled her head to his shoulder, and she cried into it, like a child out of control and he softly said, "I'm sorry baby. I'm really, really sorry.

She looked into his wet eyes, with such an expression of pain, and softly asked, "Where are they Bob?" He didn't want to say the words, but he knew he had to. "They're at the morgue, baby." She squeezed her eyes shut, not wanting to hear the words he had just spoken, and then she opened them again, "Will you go with me?" she asked, then she reached for the towel, to wipe her eyes, then Bob's. He nodded yes, and she flung the towel to the table, and they quickly walked through the door, into the hectic police station.

She was numb, while she walked through the noisy corridor, and everything seemed to be in slow motion. The world seemed different now, and nothing mattered to her, and she paid no attention to any of the commotions going on around her. As they walked, she clutched Bob's arm with both of hers, and she pulled it to her side, and clung to it, feeling the warmth and strength of his presence.

How can I live without my parents, she thought? They were everything to me. She remembered their laughter, and their zest for life, and the love they had for one another, and their love for her. She remembered the many breakfasts she cooked for James, when Joan was away on a weekend retreat with her women's group. She remembered how he made fun of her eggs, and how they laughed while he ate them. She remembered sitting by his side each morning, and watching his every move, while he devoured them, then he hugged her neck, and told her they were really very good. Then they cleared the table together, and went to a park, where he pushed her in a swing. She remembered all his jokes, and his philosophy of life. "Problems, are not inherited, they're created. If there's a problem, let's solve it and move on."

Then, as they reached the outside of the building she thought of Joan, and all of the many problems she had solved for Tina, and the way in which she understood her husband, and took care of him. Tina loved and admired the sacrifices made by her mom, sacrifices which were made for the good of the marriage, she'd say. And her zest for life itself and how she cherished every minute of it, as she constantly helped everyone around her to enjoy it also.

Tina stood on the edge of the front steps, staring into the sky. She watched the mist fill the air, and gently cover her car. An awkward sort of piece surrounded her. "Tell me it isn't true Bob." Then she sighed deeply. "I loved them so much." He pulled her to his side, and held her tight, and his eyes were filled with tears, and he replied. "I know baby, so did I." Then she looked up into his eyes, and hugged him. "I'm sorry Bob. I know you did. We loved them together.

The drive to the morgue was silent, only an occasional murmur, or sniffle, or a gasping for breath, while they were both lost in deep thought, and reliving memories of James, and Joan, the dearest people either of them had ever known.

Before long, the hospital was in sight, and Bob turned the car into the parking lot and toward the back of the building, to the entrance of the morgue and they sat in silence for a moment, neither wanting to open their doors, to begin that dreadful walk inside. She turned toward Bob, with tear filled eyes, and asked, "Oh Bob, how can this be happening?" He reached for her hand, and squeezed it, knowing the pain she felt, and wishing somehow, he could make it go away, but he knew he couldn't, and he didn't say a word, while he quickly opened his door, wanting to get this over with.

She stayed seated, and he slowly walked around, and opened the car door for her. Then, he helped her out, and he held her to his side, as he slammed the door shut. He steadied her while they walked toward the light, shining through the door window. The walk was a death walk, the sort of walk which neither of them wanted to share again. It was slow and methodical, and each step drew them closer and closer to emotional pain and duress. Tina was filled with disbelief, and somehow hoped, that this had all been a big mistake. She was silently praying that the body's they were going to identify, were not her parents at all, but instead, some other unfortunate soles, who tragically lost their lives, in a freak accident, during a terrible storm.

Bob knew the truth though, and he dreaded the thought of exposing Tina to the emotional bombshell she would soon experience. His only thoughts were to get this over with, and get the hell out of there, and try to begin the slow painful recovery from the tragedy of the day.

Bob swung the door open, and Tina gently closed her eyes, and took a deep breath, to gather her emotions, then they stepped into the lighted room, where one single figure greeted them. He was short and heavy set, probably in his late fifties, and dressed in a sloppy manner. He wore wire rimmed glasses, probably for reading, and he looked over them, as he asked if he could help them.

"Hargrove." Bob blurted out. The little man raised his eyebrows, as he replied, "Follow me please." And they followed him down a dimly lit corridor. He walked with a limp, very slowly, and it seemed like hours, and Tina wished he would hurry. They passed several doors, then he finally reached for a door knob, and he turned it, and pushed the door open, and he held it open, while they entered, the cold dark room. The far wall was lined with rows and rows of stainless steel cabinets, which housed bodies of victims of tragic accidents, or murders, or natural death, or her parents.

Tina began crying, and braced herself, hoping not to see what she had feared, while the short limping man hobbled to the cabinets in question. Bob held her tight, hoping to ward off the shock of the truth, and the man slid both drawers opened, and there they lay, so peaceful, and so still, and so silent. Her hands covered her face, and she burst into tears, then she caressed their faces and said. "Mom, Daddy. I love you so, please open your eyes, and tell me goodbye."

Bob gently pulled her away. "Come on baby." She jerked her arms free. "They're alive Bob, they're alive. Didn't you see them move?" Bob pulled her to his side, and held her tight, as he led her away. "No baby, they're gone. I'm sorry, but they're gone."

She almost came to pieces, while her and Bob walked to the front counter, then the old man slowly followed, and he walked behind the counter, and reached for the papers Tina had to sign, identifying them as being James and Joan Hargrove, of 119 Willow grove circle, Carrollton, Texas.

The old man asked which funeral home would be used, and Bob blurted out. "Harold & sons, in Carrollton."

Before Tina signed the papers, she gathered herself, sniffled, and asked, "When will they be there?" "At the funeral home?" he asked. "Yes." she replied. "First thing in the morning." He said. Tina had a strained expression on her face, as she asked, "Why so long?" The little man frowned, as he replied, "It's a state law that an autopsy be done with all traffic victims." "Why!" she screamed. The little man was becoming irritated, and he shook his head in disgust, "To check for drugs or alcohol content," he replied. Tina leaned forward, and screamed into the man's face, "Neither of them drank or did drugs. How dare you!" "Ma'am, I'm sorry, it's a state law. There is nothing I can do."

Bob rested his hands on Tina's shoulders, and turned her to face him, and stared into her crying eyes. "Honey, it can't be helped. It's not his fault. Please sign these papers, and let's get the hell out of here.
She stood silently, and stared him down. "Bob, help me, I can't do this." "Sure you can baby, just sign your name, then it will be done," and Bob gently turned her around and placed the pen into her hand, and she wiped the tears from her eyes, and signed her name.

"Good girl." Bob remarked, and then he looked at the old man, and asked. "Will there be anything else?" "No sir, that's all, and I'm terribly sorry. "Bob nodded and they left the building.

Tina balled, every step of the way, but Bob was relieved, while he guided her to the car, then he stared into her eyes, and he quickly kissed her lips, and softly spoke. "I love you." Then he opened the door, and she fell into the seat, and he closed the door, and walked around the car. His only thoughts were of helping Tina with her pain, and torment, but he realized all he could do, was to be with her, and comfort her, and time would have to do the rest. Time, he thought. It passes so slowly, when you need for it to pass quickly. Then he stared into the sky and he said a quick prayer. "Heavenly father, help us!" Then he opened his car door, started the engine, and drove away.

CHAPTER 13

Tender Moments

The drive home was awful, and Tina was exhausted, but full of questions, which Bob had no answers to. Her eyes were wet and puffy, but wide open, while she sadly asked. "Honey? Do you think they suffered? Do you think the friends they were going to meet, have found out yet? Or, do you think they're still waiting?" Bob shook his head no, and stared into her puffy eyes, when he answered, wondering, what difference does it make. "I don't know baby. I'm sure they're home by now, and no, I don't think your parents suffered.

Before long, they made a stop at Bob's house, so he could pick up some things, and then they drove to Tina's house, where they would spend the night. Her house was dark and almost spooky looking. Not one light had been left on, and Tina possessed an eerie feeling, because of its appearance. Bob unlocked the door, and reached his hand inside to turn the light on, and Tina eased past him, and turned every light in the house on, and then she plopped on a barstool, in the kitchen. He stared at her strangely, and she shrugged her shoulders, and said, "I don't want it to be dark." He smiled, while he opened the refrigerator, for a bottle of wine, and replied, "I understand, baby."

While he poured the wine, Tina said, "Shit, Bob. It seems like a nightmare, doesn't it? He stopped, and stood motionless for a moment, and then he took a deep breath, and answered, "It sure does." Tina became silent for a moment, then she spoke with a loud tone to her voice, "I can't believe it," "I just cannot believe it." He moved next to her, and handed her a glass of wine, then he grabbed a tissue, and dried her tears, but he didn't speak a word. He only watched her cry, and wished he could make the pain go away, but he knew he couldn't.

He realized that tomorrow would be a rough day for them, and while he poured them another glass of wine, he suggested they get some rest, and they sadly strolled to the bedroom. It seemed as though time had stood still in her house, while they were out, dealing with their nightmare. Her luggage was still in the floor, and the phone was on her bed, where she left it, after Bob's urgent call came. Then she moved to the window, where she had watched the storm, and gazed out of it. "You know, Bob. This is exactly where I was standing, and exactly what I was doing, during the accident. Probably the very second it happened." Tears were streaming down her cheek, and Bob moved to her side, and took her into his arms, and held her tight, then he moved her to the bed, and sat her down.

Then Tina continued, "I love the rain so much, but now, every time it rains, I'll be sad." Bob caressed her, and softly said, "Maybe for a while baby. But eventually, that sadness will turn to happiness. And you'll be glad, to have the rain, to remind you of all the happy times you shared with them." Tina threw her arms around his neck, and kissed his cheek, and then she whispered, "I love you Bob." He nervously replied, "And I love you baby."

He squeezed her hand, and stood, and then he said, "We've got to get some sleep, baby. It's one o'clock, in the morning."

She quickly sat up in her bed, and asked, "Where are you going?" "To the guest bedroom," he answered. "Oh no Bob," and she patted the bed next to her, "Please stay with me. I don't want to be alone tonight. Lie down here, and stay with me, please."

She looked sad, and desperate, and he couldn't resist, and he laid next to her, and she cuddled against him. They laid there, fully clothed, and snuggled, and Tina couldn't sleep, no matter how hard she tried. They laughed, and cried, and talked the night away about James and Joan, and how much they had meant to them, and they couldn't believe her parents were really gone. But finally, in the twilight, they drifted off to sleep.
Early, the next morning, Tina's eyes opened, and she was awakened by the sounds of dishes rattling, and the heavenly smells in the kitchen, and Bob was not by her side. She smiled, knowing what he was up to, and before long, she saw him enter the room, and he was carrying a tray of food, and on the tray, was one single rose, in a vase. His trade mark.
He smiled, when his eyes met hers, and he said, "Good morning baby." She sat up, and then he wiggled the tray over her body. She took the rose, and smelled it, and smiled, as she said, "its beautiful honey." Then she glanced at the feast he had prepared, and she felt guilty, and became embarrassed. "You must have been up all night?" "Just a little while," he replied. "It looks great, but I just couldn't eat a bite." While he poured her a cup of coffee, he replied. "I didn't think you could. But drink this, and have a piece of toast, and you can watch me eat."

He sat on the edge of the bed, and ate, while she drank her coffee. Then suddenly, he watched tears stream down her cheeks, and she said, "I can't believe they're gone Bob. Last night I thought if I could only go to sleep, that when I woke up this morning all of this would only be a bad dream." She moved her hands to her face, and cried into them, and he moved the tray to the floor, then reached his arms out for her, and she fell into them, and screamed, "Damn it! It's not a dream Bob. What am I going to do?" then she pulled away from him, and stared into his eyes, and said. "Bob, I've got so much to do today. I've got to call work, and tell them. I've got to call the cemetery, and I've got to go see my parents, and their car. Bob, I've got to see the car, and I want to go to their house. How will I ever get it all done?" And she cried, and he held her.

Then Bob spoke, "Don't worry baby. I've taken care of everything." She gazed into his eyes, and she seemed surprised, and she asked, "What do you mean?" "Well, I called Mr. Ballard at his home this morning, and he asked me to tell you how sorry he was, and for you not to worry about a thing. And I called the funeral home, and they will be ready for us at nine o'clock this morning." She glanced at the clock, and it was seven-thirty, then she interrupted him, and asked. "What do you mean; they'll be ready for us?" "Well baby, you and I can see them at nine o'clock, but everyone else, will view the caskets at two o'clock. Tina sat straight up, and screamed. "Caskets!" Goddamn Bob. They're dead. My parents are dead. What am I going to do?"

He held her, and tried to comfort her, but she cried uncontrollably, and he felt helpless, then he held her tighter. Suddenly, she pushed him away, and stood, and began walking around the room, like a caged animal, and said. "I've got to go. I've got to go see my parents." She fumbled around, trying to find something to wear, and finally settled on jeans, and a t-shirt. Bob moved next to her, and held her, and said, "Baby, calm down. There's plenty of time," and she did. Bob held Tina for a few moments as she pulled herself together and then he asked her, "Will you be alright, while I change clothes?" She nodded yes, and he kissed her cheek, then he disappeared to the guest bedroom.

While they dressed, the doorbell rang, and Bob quickly went to the door, and opened it. A smiling young deliveryman stood there, with a wreath for the door, and a ribbon for the mailbox, both from the funeral home. Then he went back to his truck, and brought out a huge floral arrangement, and Bob helped him inside.
When the deliveryman left, Bob took the card to Tina, and she read it. "May God be with you today, and every day. Thinking of you. Burgers Inc." She began to cry, and Bob held her, and they sat on the edge of the bed. "Oh Bob, that Mr. Ballard is wonderful." He wiped her tears, and looked into her eyes, and slowly shook his head yes. "You work for a great company baby. You really do," and only sniffles could be heard for a moment.

Then Bob broke the silence, "By the way, the funeral home sent a wreath for the door, and a ribbon for the mailbox. She quickly stood, and looked out her window, to see the ribbon flowing in the wind, and turned to see the time and it was eight-thirty. "Come on Bob, it's getting late, I've got to finishing dressing."

When she was ready to go, she opened the front door, and stared outside, while she waited for Bob. Her neighbor, across the street, was working in his front yard, and tears ran down her cheeks, while she watched him. Before long, Bob eased up behind her, and they stood silent for a moment. "That's something my mom will never get to do again. She loved to work in her yard so much." Bob wrapped his arm around her, while they walked to the car, and as he opened the door, for her, the neighbor saw them, and began walking toward them.

When he reached the car, Bob stood to the side, and the older man took Tina's hand. "I'm so sorry," he said. "I read about the accident in the morning paper. Is there anything I can do for you?" She looked up at him, with her red, puffy eyes, and she patted his hand. "No thank you. Everything has been taken care of. "Well dear, if you need anything, my wife and I will be here for you," and he hugged her, and shook Bob's hand, and he walked away. Bob reached down, and gave her a little hug, and whispered in her ear. "Are you okay baby?" "I'm fine. Please, let's go now."

The drive was silent, and both Bob and Tina were lost in thoughts, of Joan and James. Bob dreaded the visit to the funeral home, knowing it would be very difficult for her, but realized that after this visit, she would be stronger, and better able to deal with the events. As they drew closer, to the funeral home, he stared at her, while she gazed out the window. He wished he could help her, and take the pain away, but he knew that only time could do that, then he said a short, silent prayer. "Heavenly father. Please give Tina the strength she needs to get through this day." Then he smiled at her, as he turned into the parking lot, and parked the car, near the front door of the funeral home.

They walked to the front steps, hand and hand, and at the door, she paused, and took a deep breath, and smiled at Bob, then they entered. They were greeted by Jim Watson, the funeral director, and longtime friend of the family. Jim held his hands out for Tina, and she melted into them. He was a short, soft spoken man, and his quiet demeanor, lent itself well, to the profession he had chosen. "I'm so sorry Tina. It was a shock to everyone. Are you okay?" Tina moved to Bob's arms, and Jim and Bob shook hands, while she answered. "I don't know Jim; I just can't believe this has happened."

Jim closed his eyes, and nodded yes, and then he slowly reopened them. "It'll take time dear." And they made their way to the room, where her parent's bodies rested, and Jim said. "Tina, they look so good," and she looked toward the two caskets, and saw the face of her mom, and she rushed to the casket, screaming. "Mom. Oh mom, I'm so sorry." She cried, and caressed the face of her mom, then glanced to her right, and saw her father, and she rushed next to him, and cried out loud. "Oh daddy. How could this happen to you?"

Bob had tears in his eyes, as he watched her, then he eased up behind her, while she cried uncontrollably, and he rested his hands on her shoulders. She reached down to kiss her father's lips, and then she moved to her mother, and did the same. She was almost hysterical, and Bob held her, until she calmed down, and they stood together, side by side, and stared at her parent's bodies, with tears running down each of their cheeks.

She spent forty-five minutes, touching, kissing, and talking to her parent's bodies, while Bob stood by her side, and held her when she needed him. Eventually, she had Jim move the caskets next to one another, with a tiny isle between them, so she could see both her parents' faces at the same time. She rested her hands on theirs, and spoke to them, as if they were alive, and she laughed, and cried, and reminisced about the wonderful times they'd had and she realized that two more hours had passed.

Finally, she looked into Bob's eyes, and said. "If we're going to see the car, and go to their house, and be back here by two o'clock, we had better go now." Bob smiled, and nodded yes. His eyes were filled with tears as they left the room and then the building and then they made their way to the car. Bob was glad, glad that it was time to leave. Somehow, Tina had found a tremendous strength on this beautiful morning and with that thought and tears in his eyes, Bob dawned a secret smile as they reached the car and he opened the door for Tina

It was only a short drive to the service station, which housed her parent's car, and as Bob turned onto the parking lot, she saw the car immediately, and she screamed. "Oh my God. Bob, no wonder." Bob parked in front of it, then he reached over to comfort her, then he opened his door, and walked around the twisted piece of metal, while she stayed seated, and simply looked away. The car had been bent in half, and the front windshield was shattered where her parents were thrown against it. The top of the car was crushed, and the front tires were flat. Bob shook his head no, realizing, that had he not known, he wouldn't have recognized the car as being a Mercedes. No wonder, he thought. No one could have survived that crash, and then he returned to his car, and sat silent for a moment, while Tina took his hand, and held it.

"Let's get out of here Bob." And he started the car, and they drove away, with tears in their eyes.

It wasn't long, before they rounded the corner, of the street, which her parents' house was on. When she saw it, tears softly streamed down her face, and once Bob parked the car, she flung her door opened, and ran to the front door of the house. She quickly unlocked the door, and rushed to James' office, and sat in his favorite chair, and she rested her head on his desk, and cried out loud. "No."

Bob patted her shoulders, while she cried, but he realized she needed to be alone, so he eased into the dining room, and had a seat, and he softly cried.

Tina raised her head, and noticed Bob had left the room, and her eyes began to scan the room, and they were drawn to a picture hanging on the wall. It was a picture of Joan and James, during a ski trip they had taken, only a year ago, in Boulder Colorado. The snow had been soft; they told her, and the air crisp, and refreshing. They'd had more fun on that trip, than on any other that they could remember, and they wanted Tina and Bob to go back with them next year.

Tina snatched the picture from the wall, and she held it next to her heart, and her teary eyes, scanned the room once again, and she noticed another picture on the wall. She stood in front of it, and smiled and reminisced. It was a picture she had taken herself, one week before her parents Colorado trip. James was seated at his chair, and Joan stood behind him, with her hands on his shoulders. They had devilish smiles on their faces, and Joan had a twinkle in her eyes, as she kissed the top of his head.

Tina bent over, and kissed the picture, while it hung on the wall, and she hugged the one she held, and then she went to find Bob. He was sitting in the dining room, and she could tell he had been crying, but when he noticed her, he quickly stood, and tried to hide the tears, but she knew. She held her arms out for him, and they hugged for a moment, then she turned to him, and showed him the picture, and he smiled.

"They wanted us to go, back with them, next year," and she drew a deep breath, and then she continued. "They enjoyed that trip so much." "Well baby, we can still go next year. It might be good for us, and who knows, we might have fun too." She smiled, and led him to the den, where they sat and talked for a moment, then they strolled to the kitchen, and then to their bedroom and finally, it was time for them to leave. When they reached the front door, she turned for a final look, and squeezed Bob's arm, then they drove to Tina's house, where they changed clothes, then they went back to the funeral home.

They arrived early, and no one was there yet. Tina rushed to her parent's sides, and the caskets had been moved back to their original positions, for the viewing. She showed her parents, the picture she had taken from their wall, and told them about the wrecked car, and that she had been to their house. She straightened their clothing, and hugged their necks, and before long, the crowd began to gather, and Tina was swept away by friends and relatives, and stories of James and Joan. Suddenly, Sally's face appeared, from the crowd, and then Mr. Ballard's, and they hugged, and smiled, and cried, and talked. They stood over the bodies of her parents, and Sally rested her arm around Tina's waist, and hugged her tight.

Most of the people, in the crowd, simply paid their respects, and left, and others were seated, and stayed for a while, but by three-thirty, everyone had gone, and Tina and Bob stood alone, once again.

For the remainder of the day, only stragglers stopped by, and just before nightfall, Tina kept one of them with her, while Bob went out for sandwiches. When he returned, he and Tina sat before her parents, and ate a sloppy hamburger. Something they had done a hundred times or more, but this time, there was no laughter, and no jokes from James, and no rescues from Joan, only silence, and tears.

Tina didn't want to leave. She knew her time with her parents was limited, and she wanted to savor each moment, but the day had been draining, and finally she turned to Bob. "Honey, I guess it's silly, to sit around here all night. We can come back early in the morning. Are you ready to go?" Bob smiled and nodded yes. She was right, the day had been long, and Bob was surprised to hear her say those words, but he was glad, and he took her into his arms, and he hugged her for the longest time. She said her good-byes to her parents, and they drove home.

While they got ready for bed, Bob was in the guest bedroom, and Tina walked to the doorway, and leaned against it, then she eased up behind him, and wrapped her arms around his waist. He was startled, and he jumped, and he quickly turned to face her. "God baby, you scared me!" She held him, and cried. "Do you know, that's the first time, I've ever been able to sneak up on anyone?" And she cried out loud. "I never was able to sneak up on daddy." He held her tight, and whispered. "He was always proud of that fact, and he really enjoyed playing that little game with you."

She took his hand, and led him to her bedroom. "I really don't want to be alone. Please stay with me?" They pulled the covers back, and eased into the bed, and snuggled against one another, and they quickly drifted off to sleep.

CHAPTER 14

Goodbye for Now

At the funeral, the chapel was full, and there wasn't an empty seat, but Tina was strong, and she only broke down a couple of times. She had high emotions when the minister spoke of her parents tragic departing, and the other time, was when everyone filed past the caskets, and paid their last respects. Bob held her through the entire, emotional service, and he was there for her to lean on while they walked to the limousine, and finally, to the grave site. Bob chose not to view the bodies but instead decided to keep their image, which was in his memory, to remember each of them by.

Once the service was over, hordes of friends gathered around Tina to say their last consoling words, and she showed amazing strength, but when they left, her and Bob stood alone once again.

The gravesite was not a thing of beauty. There was no marker, or no headstone. It would be weeks before they were engraved, and put in place. For now, there were only two bare piles of dirt, to signify that someone had recently passed. The area, around the site, was gorgeous, and peaceful, and Tina was happy with that. Her parent's plots were under a huge oak tree, on top of a steep hill, which overlooked the town where they had spent their entire adult lives. There was a pond to the far right, which had ducks quietly paddling across it, and below that was a highway, full of traffic, with people going, who knows where. But beyond all of that, in the distance, stood five towering hills, which were sprinkled across the country side, to break up the monotony, of the flat land, and miles, and miles of trees, which softly flowed with the terrain.

It was a breath taking sight, and Tina only wanted to stand there, and take it all in, while she reminisced of the good times they'd had, and the joy they had shown her. Bob realized she needed to be alone, to sort out her emotions, and to say her last farewells, and to say a few prayers. Bob said a few of his own prayers, and then he quietly walked to her side, without a word, and put his arm around her waist, and pulled her close to him.

The sun was beginning to set, in front of them, and the awesome sight was too inviting to leave, and they stood there until it disappeared, and soon, the moon, and the stars took control. Then the breath taking view disappeared, and a romantic feeling took over, with the stars twinkling in the sky, and Bob pulled her closer to him, and they stood there for hours, enjoying the feeling, and recovering from the devastating tragedy of the past couple of days.

"It's a wonderful view, isn't it Bob?" "Yeah it is. It's gorgeous, and peaceful. It's perfect." "Bob do you think we'll ever get so tangled up with life, that we'll forget them?" "Honey, they'll always be close to you, and you will never forget them, you may not constantly have them on your mind, but they'll always be there, and your memories of them will never go away." Tina hugged him tight, and then he continued. "You know what, they were proud of you, and they had a great life, and you shouldn't feel sorry for them, cause they had it all, more than most of us experience in two life times." Tina looked into

Bob's eyes as she said, "I know, but I loved them so, and they were such a big part of my life, I don't know if I can ever let go." "Baby, you don't have to let go. And you shouldn't."

With that, they turned around, and slowly walked to the car, which Mr. Ballard had left for them to drive home, and they drove away. When they did, Tina turned and stared at the area, until it disappeared from sight.

By the time they reached Tina's house, she had fallen asleep, and Bob carried her into the house, and gently laid her across the bed. He sat on the edge of it, and watched her sleep for half an hour, then he undressed her, and covered her with a blanket, then he lay beside her and fell asleep, himself.

The next morning, Tina was awakened first, and she laid still for a while, staring at the peacefulness, on Bob's face, and thinking how much he meant to her, and how precious he had been the past few days, and ever since she had known him, for that matter. Then she gently ran her fingers through his hair, not wanting to wake him, and glanced at the clock. It was six a.m., and she softly kissed his cheek, and quietly eased into the kitchen to make him breakfast.

The coffee was incredible, and it was just what she needed, to get this day started. And while she cooked, she stuck her head into the bedroom occasionally, to see if he was still asleep, and he was, but by the time she finished cooking, he eased up behind her, and hugged her, with his fingers clasped, at the front of her waist, and he whispered in her ear. "Good morning baby, did you sleep well?" She turned, and gave him a little kiss. "I slept like a rock. I hadn't realized how tired I was. How did you sleep?" "Great!" he replied. Then he let out a huge yawn, and remarked. "I could have slept for another hour, but what-ever you're doing out here smelled so good, I had to investigate." Tina giggled as she said, "I'm sorry, I should have waited, I guess." Bob laughed. "Honey, I was only kidding. I don't want to sleep my life away." Tina snuggled closer to him. "But you looked so peaceful, laying there. I didn't want to bother you." Bob put his hands on his hips, like superman. "You mean to tell me, you watched me sleep?" Tina giggled, and replied, with a motherly tone. "I certainly did, and you looked so sweet."

Bob took her hand, and pulled her next to him, then he poked her ribs with his finger, and she laughed out loud, and she pulled away. "Watch it buster, that'll get you into deep trouble." Then she giggled, and attacked his ribs, and he laughed so hard, while he tried to defend himself. But she was too much for him, and he ended up in the floor, with her straddled across him, and he laughed so hard, tears came to his eyes. He finally grabbed her shoulders, and pulled her body close to his, and she gently bit his bottom lip, then she kissed it, then she kissed him, and they were whisked away for a few minutes of heated passion.

Before long, she sat up again, and gasped for air, then she pinned his shoulders to the floor, and giggled at him. "You're too much for me this morning. I just don't know what I'm going to do with you." "Beat me," he quickly replied, "Please beat me." Tina stood, with her legs straddling his body, and she reached down, for his hands, and tried to pull him up, but he was too heavy, and she giggled. "Well! You could help, a little bit, you know." While he was being raised from the floor, he laughed, and said. "But it's more fun watching you struggle. You look so serious." While she pulled, he finally made it to his feet, and they laughed, then he took her hand, and pulled her into his arms, and he softly kissed her.

When their lips parted, her eyes were searching his, and he simply gazed into hers. Eventually, she smiled, and nudged him, and then she giggled and asked, "What is it, silly?" He took a deep breath. "I haven't seen you laugh in over a week. And I missed it. It sounds like heaven to my ears, and finally, your face is glowing again, and I missed that too." Then he closed his eyes, as if to savor the moment, and she kissed his lips, then he reopened them, and he kissed hers.

She giggled, and then she began laughing out loud, and she couldn't stop. He pulled back from her, and held her by the shoulders, and he kept asking. "What's so funny?... Honey, what's so funny?" She began calming down, and she tried to tell him, while she continued to laugh, but he couldn't understand her words, and finally, she turned to the counter, and blurted out, "Breakfast is ice cold, silly. Now see what you've done!"

He hugged her from behind, and whispered in her ear, as he wiggled close to her butt. And said, "I don't give a shit!" She gasped a deep breath, "Bob? That's not like you." Then she turned, and fell into his arms, and glared into his eyes, acting as though she were upset with him. "I can't help it," he replied. She glared at him again, and fixed a stern and serious expression on her face, and she stood silent for a few seconds, then she replied, "You know what? I don't either," and they laughed, and laughed.

"It's good to laugh again," she said. "And I know momma and daddy would want me to." "That's right cupcake." A look of puzzlement jumped across her face. "Bob? No one has ever called me cupcake, except for daddy." He smiled, "I know baby. I hope you don't mind." She smiled from ear to ear. "Mind? Bob, I love it." She hugged his neck, and a tear came to her eyes, as she whispered, "And I love you."

The afternoon was spent tying up loose ends, and of course, Tina had to make a short trip to the cemetery, which was very difficult for her. She wanted to see the site one more time, without all the people, and to say her goodbyes with only her and Bob there. Bob explained, that it would get easier to go there with time, and she seemed content with that, but she wondered exactly when that might be.

Before long, it became night fall, and Bob had to work the next morning, but he had no clean clothes, and he confronted Tina. "Cupcake, I suppose I should spend the night at my place tonight, and it's beginning to get late." "No! Please. Not tonight. Why do you have to go tonight?" "Baby, I don't have any clean clothes here, and I have to work in the morning." Tina seemed frightened, and shaken by the thought of staying alone as she said, "Honey, let's go to your house and pick up some clothes, and you can stay here again. Bob, I need you."

He dropped his head and smiled, as he realized how close they had become, and how dependent they were on one another, and he loved it. But he was insecure as to why they were as dependent on one another, and he wanted them to fall in love, and not because Tina was lonely, or because she wanted to fill a void. Tina also realized her closeness to Bob, and she realized she truly loved him and enjoyed spending time with him.

She admitted, she has always wanted a relationship just like her parents had, and she knew Bob could give that to her. She remembered her daddy saying how good Tina and Bob were with each other, and she remembered her mother's prodding, for her to marry. But at the same time, she honestly felt as though her and Bob have stumbled across true love.

It's true, she thought, Sally and Jonathan had supplied me with a passionate lust that I have never experienced before, but Bob makes me feel warm inside, in a way, which no one else ever has, or ever will. I feel so comfortable around him, she thought, and I would enjoy spending the rest of my life with him. I can trust him, and talk to him about anything, and he would always be there for me, and what more could a woman want. Sex? I wouldn't know, she thought, we never have, but what if it was awful? Would it matter? I don't think it would be awful, I think it would be grand. I think it would be hot, and exciting, and I think we would lust for each other, and crave each other. I can tell, just by the way we look into each other's eyes, and hold each other, and touch each other. I don't think he would be afraid to try anything new, and neither would I.

But most of all, she thought, it's how I feel in my heart. My heart says yes, he's the one, and I believe he is, and if he asked me tomorrow, I wouldn't hesitate, I'd say yes. I would even run away, and marry him tomorrow night, if he wanted to. I love him, and I never want him to stay at his place again. I never want him to leave my side. I want to take care of him, the same way mom took care of daddy, and I want to love him, and for him to love me, and he told me that he did, and that is that.

The question is not, will we marry, rather, when will we marry? She thought, and when we do, it'll be fantastic for the both of us, I just know it will. I love the man, and he loves me, and that's all there is to it.

Bob interrupted her thoughts. "Hello, Earth to Tina. Are you there? Hello. . . .Tina?" She slightly shook her head, and refocused her vision, and then she smiled, "Oh, I'm sorry, I was just thinking" "Well, I could see that. What were you thinking?" She blushed, and lowered her head sheepishly, and then she answered, "About you. . . .And me. . . .And us." He stood, and moved next to her side, and he asked, "What about us?" She pulled away, in a devilish sort of way, and she took his hand, to lead him to the car. "Oh never mind, we'd better go, if we're going to get your clothes before morning. And they giggled. While he closed the front door, he asked again, "Oh come on, what about us?" And Tina ran through the yard, saying, "Not tonight my dear, not tonight."

Bob caught her, and he gently brought her to the ground, and they laughed and giggled under the moonlight, in the grass, and Bob said, "We're not leaving here until you tell me." Then he stared deeply into her eyes, and she said, "Okay, okay. I was thinking. . . .I love you." Bob dawned a surprised expression on his face, and he quietly said, "Baby, I've waited a long time to hear those words pass your lips."

Bob stood, and then he reached for her hand, and he slowly lifted her to her feet, then he whisked her into his arms, and said, "I love you to." Then he yelled, "Did you hear me, I Love you!" Tina was embarrassed as she said "Shh! be quiet. The entire neighborhood will hear you." He laughed, "I don't care if the whole world hears." Then he looked to the sky and opened his arms, and yelled, "I love Tina Hargrove! Do you hear me world? I love Tina Hargrove!"

She tried to cover his mouth with her hand, and they giggled, and then they laughed out loud, then their lips met, and Tina pulled him to the ground once again, and her passion was unleashed. Suddenly, Tina pulled away, and she stood, not wanting to rape him in her front yard, and she caught her breath. "Darling, we need to go." Bob stood, and they almost rubbed nosed, as he stared into her eyes. "Cupcake. I'm gonna finish this one day soon. One day very soon." They giggled, and turned toward the car, and he yelled. "Very, very, very soon." "You silly man. What am I going to do with you? Get into this car!" He laughed; his voice could still be heard as they drove away.

CHAPTER 15

Dealing With the Past

The morning was filled with sadness for both Tina and Bob, while they dressed. He was in the guest bedroom, and she sat in front of her vanity, staring in the mirror, and crying. I don't want him to go to work today, she thought, I'm not ready yet. I've got so many emotionally upsetting duties to deal with today. I have to meet with the real estate agent, and list my parent's house. That will be extremely difficult for me, even with Bob there, and now he won't be. What the hell am I going to do?

The wonderful memories of last night were just that. Memories. The laughing, the giggling, and the closeness. That was then, and this is now, and it hurts, she thought. Then she remembered how her heart was torn out, when Bob told her that he had to work today, and how empty she felt. For the first time, she realized how dependent she had become on Bob, and how much she needed him, then she realized how selfish she was, for not wanting him to go, but she couldn't help it.

Suddenly, she heard him call to her. "Cupcake? Are you dressed?" She fought the tears, and wanted to say, hell no I'm not dressed. I don't want to start this day, and have to say good-bye to you, but she didn't. Instead, she composed herself, and cheerfully answered. "Yes darling. I'll be out in a moment." "I've got to go," he called out, and she hated the sound of those words, but she knew that they were true, and that he did have to go.

When she entered the kitchen, he was reading the paper, and she came up behind him, and wrapped her arms around him, as if she didn't ever want to let him go, and she didn't, and she still couldn't believe that he was leaving. "Oh Bob don't go today. Please. Not today!" she begged. He quickly turned to her, and took her into his arms, and stared into her eyes, and softly smiled. He had a twinkle in his eyes, which made it more difficult, but she knew he hurt inside too, and that he really didn't want to leave her, but he had to. "I'm sorry baby, but I've got a client coming in from New York today, and I've put him off long enough. I have to go."

"I know you do, but it hurts so much, and I never dreamed I'd feel this way, but I do." and she softly cried, then she pulled away, and tried to gather herself. She didn't want to cry, not today. She wanted to be strong, for him, and she knew she wouldn't have her way, anyway, so what's the point of tears. Never-the-less, they did flow, then she fell into his arms, and he held her, and it felt so good. Then he raised her chin, and gazed into her eyes, and said, "But I have a surprise for you." "A surprise? What kind of a surprise?"

Before he could answer, the doorbell rang, and he looked toward the door, and then back to her, and said. "There's your surprise now." She was confused, while he walked away. What surprise? She thought. Who could it be? Then he reappeared, and behind him was Sally.

Sally, quickly walked past Bob, and held out her arms to Tina for a hug. "Sally, what are you doing here?" Sally giggled. "Bob called, and asked me if I would spend the day with you today." Then she turned to glance at Bob, and she smiled, then she turned back to Tina. "You're not ready to be alone yet." "But what about work?" Tina asked. "All of our work is being routed through Mr. Ballard today. And by the way, he sent his love, and said not to worry."

Tina brought her hand, to her forehead, in a worrisome sort of way, and Sally looked into her eyes, and giggled. "Don't worry baby, we'll have fun." But she did worry. She didn't want to spend the day with Sally, and she almost felt as though she had rather be alone, even though she loved Sally, and cherished their friendship. But it looked as though it was all worked out, and she had no choice. She glanced over Sally's shoulder, to Bob, and he smiled, and she loved what he had tried to do for her, but she felt alone, and selfishly didn't want him to go. She smiled at Sally and said. "Oh, I know we will, and I'm glad you're here."

Bob cleared his voice, to get their attention. "Ladies, I'm late. I've got to go," and Tina walked to his side, and slowly walked him to the door. She realized this would be the first time they had left one another's presence, since the tragedy, and it made her sad. When they got to the door, he hugged her, and kissed her lips, and she squeezed him, and she didn't want to let him go. He looked into her wet eyes, and said. "I'll call you every chance I get today. I'm only a phone call away, so if you need anything, please call." She nodded yes, and he disappeared to his car. She stepped onto the porch, to watch him drive away, and Sally came up behind her, and rested her hand on Tina's waist, and they waved together.

When he was out of sight, they turned from the door, and Tina melted into Sally's arms and they walked to the

kitchen, and sat on a stool and Tina cried. Sally put her arm around her, and comforted her, and said. "Baby, it's okay." Tina sniffled. "I know, and I don't mean to be childish, but I wasn't ready for this. Not yet."
Sally walked around the bar, so she could look into Tina's eyes, and she took Tina's hand, and held it, and said, "Honey, I know it hurts, but he hurts too. And believe me, he didn't want to leave you today, but he had to." Tina gazed into Sally's eyes. "I've been awfully selfish, haven't I?" Sally dawned a stern expression. "Hell no! You've been through a lot, and Lord knows, I couldn't have been nearly as strong as you, and I'm very proud of you, and so is Bob."

Tina smiled, and Sally wiped her tears away. Then Tina said, "He's been so good to me, Sally. When I needed to cry, he was there. When I needed his advice, he gave it. And there were many times, during the past week, when I wasn't nice to him at all, as a matter of fact, I was almost mean to him, almost as if I were the only one hurting. And I had almost forgotten how close he was to my parents, and how he loved them, and. . . . Damn, I've been selfish!" "You have not been selfish damn it!" Sally scolded. "I told you not to say that. He understands, and so do I and we both think you've been as strong as shit, and I don't want to hear that again!"

Tina looked surprised, to see the expression on Sally's face, and the tone in her voice. She knew that she meant it, and Tina looked at her with puppy dog eyes, and said, "I'm sorry, I know you're right. I'm just confused, and I wasn't ready for him to leave." Sally walked around the counter again, and Tina stood, and they melted into each other's arms. They hugged, and cried, but soon, the tears stopped, and they walked into the den. Tina sat in the recliner, and Sally sat in the floor, at Tina's feet, and she leaned her cheek against Tina's knee, and they sat quietly for a moment, thinking of the events of the past week. Tina finally broke the silence, with a giggle, and soon, it turned into laughter, and Sally turned, and smiled, and asked what was so funny. Before long Sally was laughing too, and she didn't know what they were laughing about, then Tina said, "You should have seen us together last night Sally. It was hilarious." Sally sat up straight, and moved closer, and smiled, and suddenly there was happiness in the house, and they were both glad, then Tina told the story.

"He tackled me in the yard, and we rolled around out there, at ten o'clock, at night and I tickled him, and he tickled me, and we laughed so hard." Sally enjoyed the happiness on Tina's face, and she laughed while Tina told the story, then Tina turned serious, and moved closer to Sally, in a confidential manner. "And Sally. He kissed me so passionately, and I almost raped him right there. He was so hot; I couldn't believe it." Sally looked at Tina, as though she were saying, and? "No, we didn't do anything, we only kissed, but what a kiss." And Tina rolled her eyes back, and fell back into the recliner. Sally was smiling from ear to ear, wanting to hear more, but Tina was lost in those wonderful thoughts, and Sally said. "You love him, don't you?" but before she could answer, the phone startled them, and Tina quickly answered it.

"Hello." And while the other party was speaking, Tina's face turned white, and she dawned a frightened expression, and she dropped the phone to her lap, and brought her hands to her face, and screamed. "No, goddamn it! No. Mom, I'm so sorry." And Sally tried to comfort her, but Tina stood, and dashed to the mantel over the fireplace, and leaned against it, and cried out loud. "What's wrong baby?" Sally asked, and she rose, and moved to Tina's side, but Tina pulled away. "Honey, who was on the phone? What was that all about?" "Oh Sally," she screamed. "I can't do it. I can't do this anymore. I just can't."

Tina moved to the sofa, and sat on the edge of it, and Sally fell to her knees, in front of her, and took her head into her shoulder, and patted her back. "What is it baby? What has happened?" Tina tried to speak, but the tears wouldn't let the words come out. Sally held her, and cradled her, and rocked her back and forth, as she said, "It's okay baby, it's okay. Finally, Tina sat up, and cleared her throat, and while she dried her eyes, she blurted out. "That was Whitney's Boat Co." And not another word had to be said. They both burst into tears, and cried their tears away as they held one another. Tina cussed, and Sally comforted her, knowing how painful the call was. Sally wished Whitney's hadn't called at all, but they did, and now, they had to deal with it.

Tina raised her head, from Sally's shoulder, and the tears streamed down her cheeks, then she smiled, when she noticed the tears she had shed on Sally's blouse, and she tried to wipe them away. "Sally, I'm sorry, I hadn't realized we cried so much." Sally smiled, as she tried to brush it away. "That's okay. Don't worry about it. It'll dry." Tina looked into her eyes, and the tears were beginning to subside. "Are you sure? You can change into one of mine, if you'd like." Sally patted Tina's hand. "No baby. It's okay, it really is." "Sally, I've got to go down there," Tina said. Sally nodded, "I know you do, and I'll take you whenever you're ready." Tina looked at her watch.

"It's eleven now, and I don't have to be at mom's house until two o'clock, how about now?" Sally stood up, and took Tina's hands, and pulled her up. "Well, let's go."

The trip to Whitney's was quiet, and Sally knew Tina's mind was working overtime, but she also knew this had to be dealt with, and despite the sadness of the moment, she was glad she could share this time with Tina, and be here for her.

When Whitney's came into view, Tina quietly shed a few tears, and they softly flowed to her lap. Sally reached over to wipe them away, and then she parked by the front door. Tina stared through the glass in the door, and motioned for Sally to do the same. "There's the asshole that sold us the boat," she blurted out, and Sally squinted, trying to make him out through the glass, but she couldn't, and they opened their car doors, then they met in front of the car, and held hands, while they walked inside.

The salesman looked up at them, when the front door closed. He smiled, in his smug little way, and as they approached him, he said. "Good morning ladies. We're preparing your boat for delivery, as we speak." Tina walked past him, and said. "That won't be necessary," and she walked up to a boat, exactly like the one Joan had picked out. "Is this it?" she asked. "Why no ma'am, yours is in the back. What do you mean, it won't be necessary? Is everything okay?" Sally quickly herded the little man to the side, and filled him in, and Tina glanced into his eyes, while Sally told him. He looked frightened, as though he didn't know what to do now. He walked over to Tina, and said. "I'm terribly sorry ma'am, I had no idea." "Of course you didn't. Take me to the boat, I want to see it." "Yes ma'am, just follow me."

As they went through the door, and into the back area, Tina spotted her boat immediately, and she rushed to it, and gently touched it, almost as if she didn't want to hurt it. She leaned her arms against it, and rested her head on them, while she cried. Sally comforted her, and then Tina turned around, and leaned her butt against it, and said, "Sally. . . .We had a great time picking this out. . . .And she was so happy. You should have seen her. . . .She was like a child." Sally became teary eyed, and replied. "I know dear. I remember that day. You were pretty happy yourself." "Why did this shit have to happen?" Tina screamed. "Why." Sally cuddled Tina as she replied, "I don't know baby, I don't know."

Suddenly, Tina stood tall, and wiped her tears, then she wiped Sally's, and they turned toward the meek, little salesman. "I want to see the manager please!" "Yes ma'am, follow me." While they walked through the store, Tina tried to gather herself, and she dried her tears, and Sally had no idea why she wanted to see the manager, but she knew Tina had good reason, and she followed her confidently.

When they arrived in front of his door, the little salesman, opened the door, and stuck his head in. "Someone would like to speak with you," and Tina heard the managers voice. "Fine," he said, and the salesman held the door for them, while they entered, then he shut it behind them and disappeared.

The manager was a nervous man, but he stood tall, while he reached his hand to Tina's for a hand shake. "Good afternoon lady's, my name is Kyle Jackson, what can I help you with?" Then he reached out for Sally's hand, and he shook it. He looked like a real wheeler dealer, with his sleeves rolled up, and his vest unbuttoned, and his loosened tie. He looked like he came straight out of a Jeff Foxworthy book, and while the girls were seated, Tina spoke.

Her eyes were red, and puffy, and it was easy to see, she had been crying, and crying for days, he thought. "Mr. Jackson. My mother bought a boat from you a month ago," and Tina turned toward Sally, as if she were looking for help and Sally scooted to the edge of her chair, and reached for Tina's hand, and she squeezed it. Tina turned toward the manager once again, and he was eagerly awaiting her reason for being there.

Then, Tina continued. "And you were supposed to deliver it to her, this coming Monday," and Tina paused, and he sat back into his chair, and lit a cigarette. "Yes, I remember," he interrupted. "Joan Hargrove, isn't it?" "That's right." Tina snapped, as if to say, don't talk about my mother with that tone. "Well, Mr. Jackson. My mother died in a traffic accident." Mr. Jackson stood immediately, and placed his hands on his desk, and leaned forward. "Ma'am, I'm so sorry." His tone rang out, as if he were saying. So, what does that have to do with me?

"Mr. Jackson, I'm here to ask you, if you could sell the boat for me?" Tina squeezed Sally's hand, then Sally brought her other hand to Tina's, and she patted the back of it. "Yes ma'am." He began to ruffle through some papers. "I only need to check the financing arrangements," and Tina interrupted. "There was no financing. She paid cash." He stopped what he was doing, and he sat down again and he smiled a sneaky little smile.

"Oh, cash, of course. Yes ma'am. I'd be glad to help you with that." Then he smiled, thinking about the additional revenue he would earn, by selling the boat. "In fact, you'll be happy to know, that this is the peak of our season, and the boat your mother selected is our hottest seller, and it should sell quickly." Tina stood, and Sally followed her lead. Tina reached out for a hand shake, and said. "Fine, thank you Mr. Jackson. I'll be waiting to hear from you." Then they turned, and left his office.

Once they were outside, Sally snuggled up to Tina's side, and giggled. You're something else, you know that?" Tina smiled, and said. "What do you mean?" Sally reached up, and brushed Tina's hair, from her face. "I don't know where you found the strength, but you damned sure handled that tycoon, didn't you?" Tina smiled, and they walked to the car, and they sat silently for a moment. Then Tina looked at her watch, and she broke the silence. "Sally, it's only twelve-thirty. Why don't we go have a drink?" Sally smiled, "Great idea, where do you want to go?" "Honey, you get around more than I do. Let's go someplace quiet." Sally held up her index finger, as if a light bulb went off in her head. "I know just the place, and its right round the corner." Tina giggled. "I had faith in you. I knew you'd know a place."

When they arrived, and were seated, the waitress came to their table, and she looked so fine. Tina slapped Sally's hand, for staring at the waitress. "Be nice," she giggled. Sally smiled, and sat up straight. "Yes mother," and she quickly glanced at the menu. "Let's see. What kind of wine would you like?" "Sally, I don't want wine today. How about scotch and water?" Sally's mouth flew open, and her eyes became as big as saucers. "Tina! I've never known you to drink scotch?" "Well, now you have." Then she turned toward the waitress, who was giggling. "I'll have scotch and water." Sally giggled, and rested her hand on the waitress's waist, and she said. "I'll just have the house wine. I guess I'm driving," and they all laughed.

While the waitress walked away, Tina scolded Sally, "Do you have to touch every woman you see?" Sally nodded, no, "Just the beautiful ones," and they laughed. "Oh Sally, what am I going to do with you. After two drinks, Tina realized it was one-fifteen, but she didn't seem to give a shit. The two scotch and waters, had calmed her down, and her mood became very relaxed. "I guess we should go, we don't want to keep, who's it, waiting." Sally roared with laughter, "Who's it. Damn, that's funny. Tina, I think, one more drink, and you'd be in another world." It was clear that Tina was beginning to slow down as she spoke, "I'm way ahead of you dear, I'm already in another world." And they stood, and wrapped an arm around each other's waist, and they left.

When they arrived, at her parents' house, the real estate lady was walking around in the yard, with her measuring tape, and clip board. She was a gorgeous lady, with short blonde hair, and a beautiful tan. She was slim, and her dress was too short for her age, but her slender legs were inviting, and Tina knew exactly what Sally was thinking, while she parked the car. Tina and Sally's eyes met, and they smiled at each other, and then they giggled, knowing what the other one was thinking, then they opened their car doors, and slid out of the car.

The lady had a warm smile, and she held her hand out for a hand shake, as she greeted them. "Hello. My name is Debra Jones, and I hope you don't mind, but I've already inspected the outside of the house."

Tina fell in love with her immediately. Her perky attitude, and spunky personality were comforting, and Tina realized she was the right person to sell this house. Tina smiled, and said, "Not at all Debra, in fact, it's refreshing."

Debra had extreme energy, and she went on and on about the beauty of the house, and the neighborhood. "It's simply beautiful out here, and so peaceful."
"Yes it is. Would you like to see the inside?"
"Certainly?" and Tina unlocked the door, and Debra hurried to the bedrooms, and Tina and Sally shrugged their shoulders, and giggled, and they tried to keep up with her.

It was easy to see, that Debra was excited about the house, and her job, and the excitement began to rub off on Tina and Sally, and they had a great time showing it to her. When all the blanks, on her form were filled out, they ended up in the kitchen, where Tina and Sally had a seat. Debra stood, on the other side of the bar, and laid her clipboard on it, then she leaned against it, and she began scribbling. Tina knew Sally was hot and bothered, and despite the age difference, she could certainly understand her attraction.

Debra's soft breasts peeked out from her dress, and Sally longed for them. They were shimmering in the sunlight, and her lips were juicy red, and looked delicious, and her magnetic eyes instantly drew you to her, and while she leaned against the counter, she had such a pleasant look across her face.

Sally continued to stare, as if she were in a trance, and occasionally, Debra glanced up at her, and she smiled, then she began writing again. When Debra finished, she reached over, and patted Sally's hand. "I guess that does it," she said. Then she turned toward Tina, "Ms. Hargrove. This is a wonderful house. And I honestly feel as though it will sell quickly, but I promise to make this easy for you," and she raised her eye brows, as if to ask. "Do you know that?" Tina closed her eyes, and nodded, then said. "Thank you." When Tina opened her eyes, she was shocked to find that Sally had leaned over to kiss Debra on the cheek, and she whispered, "Thank you." Then Debra kissed Sally's cheek, and she patted Sally's waist as she said, "I'm so glad to help."

Debra pulled out her business cards and handed one to each of them. "If either of you should need anything," and she glared into Sally's eyes. "Here's my card. Please don't hesitate." Tina giggled, and they made their way to the front door, and then to the car, and Debra began measuring the outside windows. Sally sat silently in the car for a moment, and then she opened her door again, and said. "I'll be right back." Tina became puzzled, while she watched them talk and giggled, and she wondered what in the world they were talking about. Before long, Sally returned to the car, and Debra watched her every step of the way.

When Sally slid into her seat, she almost ignored Tina, and Tina only stared at her, as she started the car. While they were backing into the street, Debra lifted her hand above her head, and wiggled her fingers bye, and Sally stuck her arm out the window, and she waved, and smiled from ear to ear.

Tina continued to stare at Sally, with an evil expression on her face. When the house was out of sight, Tina cleared her throat, and said, "Well?" Sally sheepishly glanced at her as she replied, "Well what?" "What was that all about?" she demanded to know. Sally turned her head and said, "Oh nothing." "Nothing! You two talked about something. What was it?" Sally became embarrassed, and then she became bold. Then she giggled, and she broke out into laughter, and Tina became furious, and she stared at Sally again.

"Look, I asked her out, okay?" Tina was only pretending but she seemed shocked at Sally's words as she asked, "What did you say?" Sally turned toward Tina and giggled. "I asked her out for a drink tonight, and she accepted." Tina put her hand flat against her chest, and she seemed outraged. "Sally! How could you?"

Tina glanced at Sally, and she looked so happy, and proud of herself, and Tina couldn't resist, and she began laughing, then Sally joined her. "Right in front of my face. You're one damned bold bitch, aren't you?" Sally giggled devilishly, and nodded yes. "Tina, I couldn't help myself. She was so luscious, and when she touched my hand, it almost drove me insane, and then she kissed my cheek, and I knew I had to ask." Then Tina said, "Well, I have to hand it to you, you've got more guts than I do," and they laughed about it all the way home.

CHAPTER 16

Say it Again Bob

During the next five weeks, Tina recovered from the tragedy of her parent's deaths, with the exception of occasional reminders, which brought tears to her eyes. The headstone was in place now, and grass covered the piles of dirt, and the plots began to blend in with all the others, but she visited two or three times a week, and she vowed never to forget them.

Her parent's house had been sold, and Tina donated the furniture to her parent's church. It seems that he church had a needy family, and it gave the furniture to them. Tina was proud, and she knew her parents would have been, also. Sadly, the boat had been sold quickly, and that was a trying time for her, but she knew she had no need for it, and the memories would have haunted her, so, it had to go.

At work, things were going well. The deal with The Morrison Company plowed ahead, and ground had been broken on their first restaurant, but the work continued without Jonathan. He had been caught, by his wife, with another woman, and Tina realized, it could just as easily have been her. His wife threw him out, and she filed for a divorce, and Jonathan was shamed, and he was forced out of his father's company, and he moved to California, where he apparently, had become an investment banker.

The deal with Ms. Cunningham, hadn't worked out quiet as well. She was not able to supply the restaurants, of Burgers Inc., with meat, as expected, and she worried herself into a heart attack. She survived, but she was forced to close her business, and settle down to a less stressful situation.

Sally's relationship, with Debra, was short lived, even though, they did have one exciting night together, one which Sally would cherish forever. It seems Debra had many lovers, male and female, and Sally wisely terminated the relationship, but not without shedding many tears, and having many conversations with Tina. It seemed as though Sally would never find happiness, at least not like the joy which filled Tina's heart.

Tina and Bob had developed a bond that Sally had only dreamed of and they had spent virtually every day together, since the tragedy, except when one of them was on a business trip. When they were, they were constantly on the phone. They had fallen deeply in love, and while Tina dressed for their date tonight, she smiled into the mirror, and she leaned against the vanity, and thought of Bob, and of their relationship.

He had all but taken charge of their lives now, almost as if he was the caretaker, and Tina loved it.

The passion was building for them, each of them, because they had never made love to one another, not physically anyway. But mentally, Tina had made hot passionate love to Bob on many occasions. Her imagination had taken her and Bob into a fairy tale world and she longed for the day, when that world would become a reality. That thought alone kept her aroused, and she hoped when they finally did, that they would simply move to the next level.

Suddenly, the doorbell rang, and Tina knew it was Bob, and she became excited, and she rushed to answer it. When she opened it, no one was there, and she pushed it further open and she stuck her head out, with a puzzled look on her face, for a better view, and Bob poked her ribs with his finger, and said "Boo!" Tina jumped, and made all sorts of frightening sounds, then she brought her hand to her chest to catch her breath, and she fixed an evil expression on her face, and she turned toward Bob, and she began tickling him. He laughed and laughed, till tears streamed down his cheek. "You made a terrible mistake mister!" Tina yelled. Then she joined his laughter, and they fell to the floor, just inside the doorway. They rolled around for a while, and they laughed and giggled, then they finally helped each other up, and Tina melted into his arms, and he kissed her passionately, and she kissed him back.

He eased her against the wall, then he pressed his body against hers, and she pulled him closer, wishing he was inside her, before she exploded. She raised her knee between his legs, and he squeezed them together, and he hunched it, and he also wished he was inside her, but they realized they must stop now, or there would be no turning back, and Tina didn't want sex before marriage, and Bob knew that, and simultaneously they tore themselves apart.

Tina placed both hands against the wall, and Bob turned away from her, while they both panted, and they tried to catch their breath. This is the closest they had come, ever, and it was becoming more and more difficult for them to wait, and they were hot with passion. Then Tina reached for him, and he fell into her arms, and they kissed again, then she looked into his eyes, and she gazed for a moment, and then she smiled. "God Bob. . . you are hot tonight, aren't you?" "Cupcake, you drive me wild, and sometimes I simply can't control myself." Tina smiled, and patted his cheek. "That's just the way it should be, and that's why I love you so much."

"Cupcake?" he said softly. Then she gazed into his eyes, and searched his face, before she timidly answered. "Yes darling." "Honey, I've tried to wait a respectable time since the accident," and he paused, and his eyes began searching her face. Tina knew, the moment had finally arrived, and her eyes twinkled, and joy filled her heart and her face, to make it easy for him, and then he continued. "Honey, I love you. And when I'm around you. . . .Well, I've paid close attention to us the past couple of months. And baby, we are perfect for one another." And Tina didn't say a word; she only smiled with anticipation, and waited. "Tina, darling, well, you know how I feel about you, and well, shit..." Then Tina giggled and put her finger to Bob's lips to stop him from further embarrassment and she stared into his eyes and she put her hand on his chest and she quickly, and very matter of factly, said, "Bob, will you marry me?"

Bob only dropped his head and he began to shake it no, as he said, "Was it really that bad?" Tina laughed out loud as she said "Baby I can't decide if I should *ever* tell anyone just how awful that really was.

Then Bob found the seriousness of the situation and he stared deeply into Tina's eyes as he said, "Baby, please don't interrupt me, cause I've got a lot to say to you, OK?" Tina dawned a serious expression as the surprise of Bobs works overtook her, and she silently shook her head yes.

Bob steered Tina to a chair on the porch, as he held her hand, and he dropped to his knees. He was silent for a moment, as tears filled his eyes, and Tina felt his tenderness as he was readying himself. Then her eyes began to fill with tears and Bob cleared his voice before he began to speak.

"Cupcake, we have known each other for a long time now and I cannot believe that we are finally here at this moment in time, doing what we are doing, but we are." Then he paused before he continued. "Do you remember the year that you, and I and your parents went on that camping trip to the Rocky Mountains in Denver?" Tina nodded yes, and then Bob pushed on. "I was going to ask you on that trip if you would, you know, marry me, but you began talking with James about this guy that you had met, Stephen or something, whatever.

Then Bob paused again as he tried to compose himself. "Well, I have waited for this day, since that day. This is like a dream for me. I have loved you since the day that I first met you." Then Bob asked, "Do you remember that day? As tears began to stream down Tina's cheeks, she nodded yes, and Bob said, "I believe, on that day, I learned that you liked ice cream, chocolate ice cream. In fact, I learned that you were having a love affair with chocolate ice cream." And

Tina smiled and said, "And I still am." Bob snickered and said, "Yep, you are."

"But, he said, at the time, I was busy with what's her name, and it would have been impossible. But now, it's not impossible, now, it's within reach and now is the time."

Bob touched Tina's hair as he said, "You know baby, I love this long black hair on this beautiful head of yours." Then he moved both of his hands to her face as he caressed it and the tears were flowing from Tina's eyes but she had a loving and sincere expression on her face, as Bob said, "And this face is something to die for and I have enjoyed looking into those happy eyes of yours for all of these years." And both of his thumbs gently wiped the tears away. Then he placed his index finger on her nose and he said, "Awe yes, your perfect nose", then he touched her ear, "And these ears and this chin and those sexy thin lips of yours." And Bob reached up and gently gave Tina a kiss on them, and Tina kissed him back.

Then, Bob touched Tina's chest as he said, "But, it's your heart, and he tapped on her chest as he continued, "That I cannot resist. You, my dear, have the biggest heart of anyone that I know and I not only fell in love with it, but I truly admire that about you."

Then Bob was coming in for the kill and Tina felt it and knew it and she cherished it.

They both starred each other down as Bob said, "Cupcake, I love everything about you as deeply as I have ever love anything or anyone on this earth. And I need you baby, for me to be a complete man, I need you." Then Bob held her hand a little tighter as he said, Cupcake, would you marry me. Would you be my wife as well as my friend and my lover?" And Bob brought a gorgeous wedding ring from his pocket and flashed it in front of Tina's eyes as he spoke those words.

A rush of excitement surrounded Tina as she heard those words come from Bob's lips. It had finally happened. She would become Mrs. Tina Evans, and she was thrilled, and she didn't need to say a word, because Bob could see the answer written all over her face, but she did anyway. She hugged his neck, and yelled "Yes! Yes! Yes! I certainly will, I will, I will. I love you Bob and I'll be a damned good wife to you!" The excitement spilled over to Bob, as he slipped the diamond onto Tina's finger and his smile said it all. They were finally to be married, and that was all he had ever wanted, and dreamed of, and finally, it would happen, and he knew she was right for him and him for her. They hugged, again and again, then she pulled him to the kitchen, and sat him on a barstool, and she looked so inviting, and lovely, and happy.

"Oh darling, you have made me so happy." And she raised his hand, and she kissed it, and he giggled. "When?" she asked. He was thrilled by her excitement, and he couldn't stop smiling at her as he answered, "Anytime at all. Tonight, tomorrow, next week, next month." She hit his arm. "You're not much help!' and they laughed out loud. "Let's see, she said, today is Saturday. How about two weeks from today? That'll give me enough time to get everything arranged, and won't give you much time to change your mind." They laughed, and then she began asking a barrage of questions. "Where do you want to get married?" Then she paused, and took a breath. "I just can't believe it.

Mrs. Tina Evans." Then she continued, and Bob giggled at her. "What type of ceremony do you want? Or do you want one at all? Let's just run away." Bob looked at his watch, and said. "Cupcake. Right now, we need to run away to the restaurant. It's getting late." Tina stood, and said. "Oh, I'm sorry, but it's entirely your fault, you hunk." She caressed his cheek, and she softly kissed the other one, then she took his hand, and she led him to the door.

During the entire drive to the restaurant, the two of them played a sexy little game of pik-a-boo. As Bob drove, she stared at him, but suddenly he felt her stares and glanced at her and she quickly looked away. Then she looked out the window of the car and he stared at her until she felt his stare and she glanced at him, but he quickly looked away, then they both smiled, then they laughed out loud. Finally, Tina poked Bob in the ribs and he almost jumped out of the car. Happiness filled the air as the two lovers drove toward dinner.

When they arrived at the restaurant, Tina leaned close to the waiters' ear, while he seated them, and she whispered to him. "We're getting married in two weeks." He stood back, and looked at Bob, and smiled. "Congratulations," he exclaimed, and Bob nodded, then he stared at Tina with loving eyes. "Do you have to tell everyone?" "Yes, I do. I'm so happy, I want everyone to know." And Bob leaned back in his seat, and he smiled at her, and he looked her over. "You're one beautiful lady. And I'm one lucky man."
A serious expression crossed Tina's face, as she asked. "Bob? What about children? Do you think we're too old?" "No, we're not too old! What do you think, baby?" "Well. I don't know. I do know though, if I were pregnant today, when the baby was ten, I'd be

forty-eight, and you'd. . . .Well, you'd be older," he giggled. "Does that matter to you?" he asked. "I think so. Yes, it does, as a matter of fact," she replied. "Well then, we won't have any." "But Bob, I thought you wanted children?" "Cupcake. I wanted you, and now I'm finally gonna have you. If we have children or not, it makes no difference to me, as long as I have you."

Tina took his hand into hers, and she scooted closer to him, then she leaned over to kiss his cheek, and then his lips, and then she threw her arms around him, and she kissed him passionately, and he gasped for air, and laughed. "Being your husband will be a real experience, I can see that now."

"Sweetheart, where are we going on our honeymoon?" Bob leaned back in his chair. Oh I don't know. How does a cruise down the Riviera sound?" Tina squealed, and she stood, then she hopped into his lap, and she hugged his neck, and kissed his cheek, and everyone in the restaurant turned toward them, but she didn't care. "Oh Bob! That's perfect. I love you so much." Then she whispered into his ear. "Can you wait that long, before we make love?" "I don't know," he uttered, and they both giggled. Tina whispered into Bob's ear, "I can't wait to get a hold of you," then she giggled, and continued. "And I certainly can't wait for you to get a hold of me either." They both laughed, and she whispered. "It'll be so great, and I get hot just thinking about it." She was beginning to drive Bob wild, and she knew it, and he responded. "Baby, I've imagined that for fifteen years, and you're right, it will be great."

Tina returned to her seat, and they held hands, like teenagers, and a silence fell over the table, and smiles crossed their faces, while they listened to the soft music, and imagined their lives together. Mr. and Mrs. Evans. Together. Forever.

CHAPTER 17

A Dream Come True

The two weeks flew by much quicker, than Tina had realized, and while she and Sally sat in her office discussing the wedding plans, Sally laughed out loud. "What's so funny?" Tina asked. "Oh, after all this time, it'll seem odd to call you Evans, instead of Hargrove. Are you going to give me much time to adjust?" Tina smiled. "Sure, take as much time as you need. You can even take two days, if you need to." They laughed, and laughed, then Tina gathered herself, and brought her mind back to the details of tomorrow's wedding.

"Everything is working out well!" Tina remarked. "I'm glad we decided to get married in my parent's church and with you as my maid of honor, and Mr. Ballard giving me away, I'll have some memories I can be proud of. Suddenly, a sad expression streaked across Tina's face, and she stared off into space.

"What is it sweetie?" Sally asked. "I wish my parents could see this. They loved Bob so much, and it would have thrilled them to see us marry." "I knew it would be difficult happy but difficult day for you baby, but you're right. They would have been thrilled, and proud, and so am I, and so is everyone who knows you. All I had to do was see you in your wedding dress the other day. You looked delicious, and pure, and happy. And I know I'm going to envy you tomorrow, and I almost wish it was me instead." Sally smiled, while she talked, and sat on the edge of Tina's desk.

Tina gazed into her eyes, and she giggled. "You're a piece of work, do you know that?" Sally raised her hand to her chest, and replied. "Me? Whatever do you mean?" Tina patted Sally's knee. "Okay. I'm gonna sound like someone's mother here, but here goes anyway. You are so damned good looking. Yet you're so damned attracted to women, and it would be so simple for a gorgeous woman like you to find a man like Bob, if you would only let yourself. So, don't envy me. Please don't. Be happy for me, but don't envy me."

"Gosh mom, that's pretty heavy stuff, is there anything else?" Tina stood, and giggled, and took Sally's hand into hers, and she kissed Sally's cheek as she said, "Yeah, just one little thing. Don't hustle all the good looking women at my wedding tomorrow!" They laughed, and hugged, and Sally looked at Tina, as if to say, help me! Then she said. "I can't resist. I don't know what it is, but I don't feel the same with men, as I do with women." Tina nodded yes. "I can see that." "There's just something about watching a woman walk across the room," Sally continued.

Tina could see Sally visualizing another woman as she spoke, "They're seductive, and hot, and soft, and their lips are so sweet, and luscious. They're much gentler than a man, and they know just where to touch you, and how to touch you, and how to caress, and slowly enjoy. And whether she's undressing me or I'm undressing her, the turn on is incredible. And when we lay next to one another, her skin is soft, and hot, and you can almost feel her throb, and you know that she wants you, and we can enjoy one another all day long, not just briefly, like with a man, but all day long."

Then her eyes opened, and she saw Tina staring at her, then Tina giggled. "You really get into this shit, don't you?" Sally smiled, and nodded yes. Tina continued to stare into Sally's eyes and she quietly and gently said, "Sweet heart, she is coming for you. I don't know who she is, but she will be there for you just as Bob is there for me." Then Tina continued, "You know what? I don't know who she is, but I can tell you this. She will be one lucky bitch." Sally snickered and nodded, as if to say, I know, I know.

"Well baby." Tina said. "As much as I'd love to stand here, and talk with you about seducing other women, I've got a wedding to prepare for. You're still coming to my house tonight, to help me pack, aren't you?" "I wouldn't miss it for anything," she replied with an excited smile. "Okay, I'll see you then, and by the way. Get some work done this afternoon!" They laughed, and Sally stood, for a hug and knowing that Sally was watching, Tina teased her, with a seductive walk to the door, then she stopped, and she winked, and she blew Sally a kiss over her shoulder, and as she walked through the door, they heard each other laughing.

During the drive home, Tina's mind was flooded with many thoughts of the wedding. She couldn't believe that in less than twenty-four hours, she would become Mrs. Bob Evans, and that today, would be the last day that she would be a Hargrove. Two wonderful weeks, she thought, no work, no problems, and no nothing. Just love, happiness, and pleasure.

She'd never been on a cruise ship before, and she wondered what it would be like. She could imagine her and Bob seeing all the sights, and laughing and giggling, and having a great time. Then she imagined them having a quiet dinner, and dancing the night away, then retiring to their cabin, for a night cap, and a night of passionate love making, and when they finished, they'd do it all again. We'll make love in the morning, she thought, then after lunch, and before dinner, and maybe after dinner, I'm not quite sure about that one yet, and she giggled. Then after dancing, and after our nightly walk on the deck, and absolutely, after our night cap, especially then.

She was taken away with those thoughts, and then she began to imagine normal everyday life. Life after the honeymoon, after the celebration, after the glitz and the glamour. Routines, she thought. How boring. Not for us. Routines are for other people. And suddenly, she felt responsible for that, as if their happiness were her responsibility, and her duty. Our lives have to stay fresh, she thought, and happy, and exciting, and if we even suspect a routine coming on, we need to make a change immediately. No, she thought, we will make a change immediately, just like my parents did. I know, most people say that, but we'll do it. We have to. It's got to stay exciting, she thought. How can I keep it exciting?

She wrestled around with that one for several minutes, and she thought of many things she could do, to keep their relationship hot and exciting. Let's see, there's breakfast in bed, sexy night gowns at bedtime, I could read about happy, healthy sex, and be there for him, when he comes home from work, we can take trips, enjoy friends, go dancing, and do this, and do that.

Then, as she turned into her driveway, it hit her. Almost like a light bulb, blinking in the night, and she smiled from ear to ear, and even giggled. None of this matters! Not one damned bit! The one thing which we have in common, the one fiber which draws us to one another, and keeps us coming back for more, the one thing which we adore about each other, and cherish the most in life, is laughter. It's that simple, she thought. We've got to keep laughing.

Oh, I love to hear him laugh, and he's said the same about me, and we can't ever get so tangled up with life, that we forget how to laugh. A warm feeling rushed through her body, as she realized, that laughter was the answer, to a long and happy marriage. The key, to unlocking Bob's joy, and hers, was laughter, and she turned her car off, and she sat there for a moment, and enjoyed the feeling. Then she realized that, at this very time tomorrow, she would be whisked away into a new life, with new adventures, new expectations, and a new love in her heart, one which she would proudly carry around with her, for the rest of her life. She adored Bob, and he her, but above all, they shared the gift of laughter, and she would use that tool, as the cornerstone of their marriage, the centerpiece, the focal point, and the strength.

After she checked the mail, and unlocked her front door, and swung it open, she realized, this was the spot where Bob had proposed to her. She smiled, as she thought, right here in this very spot, this is where it happened, less than two weeks ago. This is where that dear, sweet man uttered those words. His eyes were as big as a saucer, she remembered, and he was timid and shy, almost frightened. With sad, puppy dog eyes, almost afraid of rejection, he asked me to marry him, and I was swept away, and I still am, and I can't wait to begin our new lives together, as Mr. and Mrs. Bob Evans.

Tina wrapped her arms around herself, and she held herself, as those wonderful thoughts, floated through her mind, and she smiled, and realized she had made the right decision. She touched the walls, as she moved down the hallway, and she soaked in all the fabulous feelings of that faithful night, and she wondered if Bob was having the same feelings as her.

When she entered the bedroom, she thought. This is where we'll sleep together, where we'll make mad passionate love together. We'll laugh and cry in here, and hug and kiss, and if we ever have an argument, God forbid, this is where we'll make up. She smiled, and giggled, and laughed, and felt the warmth, as those thoughts drifted through her mind. Then she conceded, at least we'll live here temporarily, until we decide exactly where we do want to live.

Why wouldn't we want to live here, she thought? It's beautiful here. The bedrooms are large and comfortable. The kitchen is laid out perfectly. The den is cozy and warm. The deck is gorgeous. The trees and grass are beautiful, and the view, on top of this hill, is breath taking, but still, I want Bob to be happy. If he wanted to sell this house, and move, I'd find some boxes, and pack, at a moment's notice.

Then she fell into the bed, and thumbed through the mail, and there was a card from Bob, and she took it, and she sit up, and ripped it open, and it said. The next time I see your wonderful smile and twinkly eyes, it'll be minutes before we say, I do. I just wanted to tell you now. I do! I love you cupcake. Bob. . . .A soft tear came to her eyes, as she fell back into her pillow, and she yelled. "God, I love him! I love him so much!" I wish he was here now, I'd hug his neck, and kiss. . . . Damn, he's a neat guy!

Tina's entire afternoon was spent with those wonderful thoughts, and she didn't get a single thing done, except read her card over and over again, and she really didn't give a shit, whether or not she accomplished anything. Then her doorbell rang, and it was Sally, and when Tina opened the door, she hugged Sally's neck, then she rested her hand around Sally's waist, and she pulled her close to her, while they walked down the hallway, and then to the kitchen.

"Coffee, or wine?" Tina asked. "How about wine?" Sally replied. "By the look on your face, it's going to be a long night." And they laughed. "Sally, look at this," and she showed her the card Bob had sent. "Just look at what that precious man sent me." Tina stared, and smiled with anticipation, while Sally read those beautiful words, then they hugged, and Sally said, "What a hunk. You had better take care of this man, or someone else will!" Tina giggled, "Who you?" then Tina laughed. "I'm sorry; he's not your type." Then she cupped her hands underneath her breasts, and she lifted them. "He doesn't have any of these, and between his legs, he has a. . . . Well, he has more than we do." And they laughed, and Tina tried to speak, but the laughter overtook her, then she blurted out. "And he's not soft, he's hard. Believe me; he's very-very hard." And they laughed again, and tears came to their eyes, then finally, the laughter began to fade, and they caught their breath.

As they were holding one another, Tina stared into Sally's eyes, and a stern, serious expression overtook her, and she said. "Sally, I love him, I really do, and we're gonna be so damned happy." Sally held up her hands, and said. "Hold it! Hold everything! You don't have to tell me," and she giggled. "It's written all over your face, but more important than that, I just saw Bob a few minutes ago. And he's just as loony ass as you are, and he said the exact same words. We're gonna be so damned happy." She giggled again. "Did you guys dream that line up together?" "You saw him?" Tina bellowed. "Where?" Sally quickly answered, "After work, down in the parking garage." Tina wished it had been her in the garage with him, and then Sally went on. "Yeah, he put his arm around my waist, and it really shocked me. Then he pulled me into his body, and he stared into my eyes, and he's so strong, as you know. You didn't tell me he was so strong Tina, and he kissed my lips, and Mr. Watkins had to come pry us apart." Then she laughed out loud, and Tina hit her shoulder, then she joined Sally's laughter, and they hugged, and Tina said while she was laughing, "Honey, I'm not worried about you, you're beautiful and gorgeous, but like I said, he's not your type."

"Enough of this shit. We've got work to do," Tina ordered. "We've got two weeks' worth of clothes to pack, and we had better get busy." Sally saluted, and they giggled, as they marched to the bedroom.

They laid Tina's luggage on the bed, and they slowly filled each of them, but they talked and laughed and giggled about each piece of clothing before it was packed. They decided when and how each piece should be worn, then they came to the clothing which Sally had helped Tina select at Carmella's. They acted as if, each piece was too hot to handle, and as though it burned their hands to hold them, then they dropped it, and blew on their hands, and then they did it again and again.

They laughed the night away, and soon, everything was all packed, and they double
checked, then triple checked everything, and soon Sally was gone, and a hush fell over the house, and Tina became excited, about tomorrow. Only fourteen short hours away, she thought. "I can't stand it anymore; I've got to tell him goodnight." And she picked up the phone, and dialed his number, and she listened to each ring, very carefully, as if they held some sort of significance.

On the fourth ring, he picked up, and she heard his sleepy voice. "Hello," he said. "Hello darling. Did I wake you? I'm sorry, but I couldn't help myself. I had to call and say goodnight. Yes, I got your card today. You're so sweet, thank you. I know it won't be long, only fourteen more hours, and you'll be mine. That's right, in fourteen hours, I'll be yours too, but then, I'm already yours. Bob, listen to me. I've got something very important to tell you. Are you listening? . . . . I love you! . . . .Oh honey. When you say it, it sounds so wonderful. Get some sleep, and I'll see you soon. I probably won't sleep either. Goodnight darling. I love you. Bye-bye." And Tina brought the phone to her breasts, and she hugged it, for a moment, then she hung it up.

She undressed, and pulled the covers back, on her bed, and she wiggled into her it, but she couldn't sleep. She tossed and turned most of the night, not from worry, but from anticipation, and the excitement of it all. For some reason she didn't give a shit if she ever slept, she only wanted to get this night over, and become Mrs. Bob Evans. Then she knew that she would have no problem with sleep, or rest. Then she would have piece, and love, and joy, and satisfaction. Then she would have it all!

At five a.m. she finally found sleep, but it came far too late, and her phone rang at seven a.m., and it was Bob. "Hello Cupcake. Are you awake yet?" "Oh baby, I don't think I've been asleep yet. You sound so full of energy; you must have slept well? I missed you last night too. Did I ever! I hope we never have to do that again. Hey, do you realize that tonight when we go to bed, I'll be Mrs. Bob Evans, we'll be on a cruise ship, and you'll be lying beside me." Bob interrupted. "Or on top of me, that's right," and she giggled. And we'll never be alone again. Wow. I love you Mr. Evans. I've got to go, and I'll see you in. . . . oh. . . .about seven hours. Ha, ha. Bye-bye. I love you.

It didn't matter that she hadn't slept last night, she was getting married today, and she hurried to the kitchen for some delicious hot coffee, and it was hot, and she loved it, and it woke her up, and brought her back to life. She realized, it would be the last morning cup of coffee, she would have as a Hargrove. After this day, she'd be an Evans, and she said it again, and again, Tina Evans. I love it she thought, I simply love it.

Sally stopped by, at ten AM since her and Tina were going to drive to the church together. They loaded the luggage early, and then they sat around, and laughed, and cried, and giggled, and talked about old times, until twelve-thirty. Then Sally looked at her watch, and stood, and asked Tina if she was ready to go. Tina became nervous, and she quickly stood, and she asked. "Is it time already?" And she acted as though she was going to the guillotine instead of to the altar. She took a deep breath, and said, "I'm ready," and they drove away.

Tina was nervous the entire trip, and finally Sally spoke. "Honey, will you calm down. Yes, Bob will show up, the preacher will be on time, and everything will be fine. Quit worrying, that's my job." Then she turned to Tina and giggled. "Let me do my job, will you?" and they laughed. "I'm sorry. I haven't had much practice at this." "Wait a minute," Sally giggled. "You only get to do this one time, and no one gets to practice," They laughed again. "Thank you for being here Sally I'll be okay," Tina said. "Well, you better be. Because if you're not, well, I guess I'll have to marry Bob," Sally jokingly said. Tina shook her head no. "That's okay, that's okay. I'll manage."

Then the church appeared in the distance, and Tina stared at it, and said. "It's beautiful isn't it?" "Yeah, but not as beautiful as you're gonna be, when we get you into that beautiful dress of yours," and she winked at Tina.

When they pulled up to the side entrance, the minister's secretary, Ms. Smithers' was there to greet them, and she directed them to Tina's room. She was a cheerful, heavy set lady, in her fifties, with short graying hair, but she was well dressed, and her dress flowed down to her feet. Her personality was perky, and her breath was taken away when she saw Tina's wedding gown. They hung it over a door, in the tiny room, and Ms. Smithers disappeared, and Tina collapsed on the sofa. "Are you going to make it?" Sally asked. Tina laughed, and replied, "With bells on."

"Oh, speaking of bells, I'm gonna let you rest for five more minutes, then you're getting dressed. It's one o'clock, and I cannot wait to see you in it again," Sally said with a childish look on her face. Tina held her hands to cover her face. "Oh Sally, you embarrass me." "Yeah, right," Sally said, and Tina stood, and raised her arms to the ceiling, and said. "Why wait? Dress me, my dear." Sally became excited, and she raised the wedding gown, from the half opened closet door it hung on, and she draped it across the long sofa, and Tina quickly peeled her sweat shirt and blue jeans off. As she stood there, Sally became motionless, as her eyes scanned Tina's luscious body, and she said. "Oh baby. Shit!!!" Tina smiled, as she interrupted Sally. "Forget it Sally, this body is spoken for." Sally just shook her head, as if to say, that's too damned bad, then she lifted the beautiful dress over Tina's head, and Tina wiggled into it.

It was a gorgeous flowing white satin dress, with a four-foot train, and it had a seductive white, see through, mesh from her shoulders, to her breasts, and they glistened through it, and the sight drove Sally wild, but Tina would not let her touch. When Sally zipped it, from the back, the dress hugged every curve of Tina's gorgeous body, and it gave her an irresistible and tantalizing look, but Tina playfully slapped Sally's hands, and said. "No, no. Be nice." Sally giggled as she replied "I'd love to, if you'd stop slapping me.' And they giggled together. The Vail was made of the same white see through mesh, and the top of it was covered with soft pastel colored flowers.

Once Tina was dressed, Sally seated Tina at the vanity and she slowly brushed Tina's long black hair, and Tina loved the pampering, and she didn't want Sally to stop, but time was growing short, and finally, Sally moved across the room, and asked Tina to stand. When she did, and turned to face her, Sally's eyes grew as big as saucers, and her breath was taken away. "Oh honey. You're absolutely incredible." Tina lowered her head, in an embarrassing sort of way, and asked, "Do you really think so?" "Oh baby, I certainly do." And Sally walked next to her side, and she took Tina's hand, and said. "Bob is one lucky man, and I mean that from the bottom of my heart." Tina replied softly, and sincerely. "Thank you Sally, that means a lot to me."

Before long, there was a knock on the door, and it was Ms. Smithers, and she had come for Tina. "It's time dear." Then Sally glanced at Tina, and said. "You are without a doubt, the most beautiful bride I have ever seen," and Tina knew she meant it. Then the photographer began taking pictures, and Sally snuggled up against Tina, and Tina took Sally's hand, and she whispered into Sally's ear. "Thanks Sally. I love you." Sally smiled, and said. "I love you too. And good luck." They squeezed each other's sweaty hands, and they began their long walk to the door leading to the chapel, where they met Mr. Ballard.

He looked wonderful, and dignified, and prestigious, and gracious. And he took Tina's hand, and he softly kissed it, and said to her. "I shouldn't be surprised. You look like an angel. Tina, you're lovely, and you make me proud." The music Queue began and he asked. "Are you ready dear?" She smiled, and took a deep breath, and nodded yes, then she leaned over to kiss Sally's cheek, and she stood tall, while the doors to the chapel were opened.

The chapel was gorgeous, and overflowing with people and Tina heard the oohs and the awe's and saw the smiles when she appeared before everyone. There were beautiful flowers dawning the entire room, but the real beauty was at the very end of the isle. It was Bob's inviting smile, which made it all worth it. He stood there so proud, as he anticipated her arrival. He had the expression of a man, who had just won the lottery, and she was the prize, and she knew he was happy. Her beautiful smile was only outweighed by her shimmering dress, and she and Mr. Ballard began the long slow walk to her lover, her best friend, and her husband, Bob Evans.

With each step, they were drawn closer and closer to one another, and the excitement built. Tina and Bob gazed into each other's eyes, and their smiles became a permanent fixture on their faces, and her heart pounded, and she was sweating, and she wondered if he was too. This had to be the next best thing to sex, she thought, and she was afraid she might climax before this ceremony was over.

She felt lovely, as her and Mr. Ballard continued their walk down the aisle, and Bob was getting closer, and her smile covered her face, and she was happier than she had ever been before. Bob's eyes twinkled in the lights, and he also looked like an angel, and Tina couldn't wait until tonight, when they were alone, and on the ship. She'd show him then, but for now, he looked so strong, and she felt so weak. Please Bob, she thought, come for me now. I need your help, and support. Hold me, cuddle me, caress me, sweep me off my feet, and take me away, like in my dreams. Please Bob, come take me now, but she knew he couldn't, and she nodded to the crowd of friends, and relatives, then she turned her eyes back to Bob, and his were fixed on her, and he couldn't take them off her.

Bob was so close now, she could almost reach out and touch him, and she wanted to so bad, but she didn't, she simply continued to slowly walk, knowing she would be by his side very soon, only a few more steps, she thought, and then she was there. Bob took her hand, and he whispered into her ear. "You're beautiful cupcake. I love you." She kissed his cheek, and said. "I could eat you up, and I will later. You just wait." Then she gave him a devilish little smile, and she knew he was hot, and so was she.

They smiled at the minister, as he spoke the words which Tina knew that she would hear this year, but never in her wildest dreams, did she realize that it was Bob Evans who would be standing next to her.

Thoughts of her parents began to flood her mind, and she knew they would have been proud of her, and of Bob, and she wished they were with her now, and she shed a tear for them, then one for her. Bob saw the tears, and he reached to her eyes, and he wiped them away, then he squeezed her hand, as if to say, I love you, and I will take care of you, for the rest of our lives, and you can count on me, I will always be there for you.

Tina turned to him, and she smiled, then she mouthed the words, thank you, and she squeezed his hand, as if to say, I love you too, and I will take care of your needs, for the rest of our lives, and you can also count on me. I will always be there for you too.

Then Tina heard the minister utter the words she had longed to hear. "Do you Bob Evans, take this woman. . . .And she smiled, and closed her eyes, and she thanked God for this moment, and for Bob. Then Bob turned to face Tina, and she heard his sweat reply. "I do." And she remembered his card from last night, when he stated he did, and that he always would, and she was proud. She couldn't wait to answer the same question, and to slide the rings onto each other's fingers.

Finally, it was her turn, and the minister uttered the same words to her. Do you Tina Hargrove, take this man. . . .She stared deeply into Bob's eyes, while the minister spoke, searching for the love he had for her, and it was easy to find, and his eyes twinkled. When the minister had finished, Tina blurted out," I certainly do!" And they turned, to face the minister, to hear those beautiful words, which would finalize the entire event. "I now pronounce you man and wife. Mr. Evans, you may kiss the bride."

Bob gently lifted her Vail, and her eyes scanned his face, and she smiled a devilish little smile, then he drew her close to him, and their lips met, and Tina passionately kissed him. He was startled for a moment, then he responded with a passionate kiss of his own, and they gave the crowd a moment to remember. While they kissed, each person in the crowd recognized the deep love that they held for one another, and the crowd admired the two, for not being bashful about showing it.

With that kiss, Tina realized she had finally done it. She had finally married, after thirty-seven years, and she was swept away with those thoughts. Their lips parted, and they stood motionless for a moment, smiling, and gazing into each other's eyes, then Tina said. "I love you, Mr. Bob Evans," and he quickly replied. "And I love you, Cupcake," and they giggled.